To Kill a Mockingbird

Harper Lee

**Oxford
Literature
Companions**

OXFORD
UNIVERSITY PRESS

Contents

What are Oxford Literature Companions?

Oxford Literature Companions is a series designed to provide you with comprehensive support for popular set texts. You can use the Companion alongside your novel, using relevant sections during your studies or using the book as a whole for revision.

Each Companion includes detailed guidance and practical activities on:

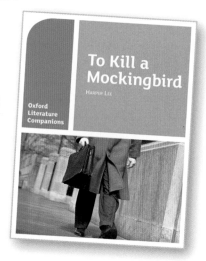

- **Plot and Structure**
- **Context**
- **Characters**
- **Language**
- **Themes**
- **Skills and Practice**

How does this book help with exam preparation?

As well as providing guidance on key areas of the novel, throughout this book you will also find 'UpGrade' features. These are tips to help with your exam preparation and performance.

In addition, in the extensive **Skills and Practice** chapter, the **Exam skills** section provides detailed guidance on areas such as how to prepare for the exam, understanding the question, planning your response and hints for what to do (or not do) in the exam.

In the **Skills and Practice** chapter there is also a bank of **Sample questions** and **Sample answers**. The **Sample answers** are marked and include annotations and a summative comment.

How does this book help with terminology?

Throughout the book, key terms are **highlighted** in the text and explained on the same page. There is also a detailed **Glossary** at the end of the book that explains, in the context of the novel, all the relevant literary terms highlighted in this book.

How does this book work?

Each book in the Oxford Literature Companions series follows the same approach and includes the following features:

- **Key quotations** from the novel
- **Key terms** explained on the page and linked to a complete glossary at the end of the book
- **Activity boxes** to help improve your understanding of the novel
- **UpGrade** tips to help prepare you for your exam

To help illustrate the features in this book, here are two annotated pages taken from this Oxford Literature Companion:

Key quotations from the novel

UpGrade tips to help prepare you for your exam

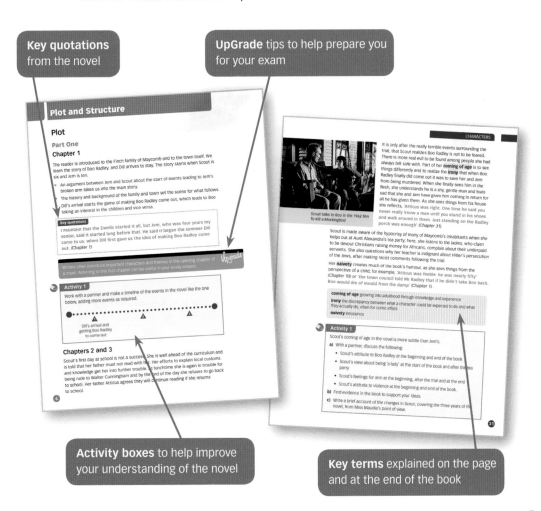

Activity boxes to help improve your understanding of the novel

Key terms explained on the page and at the end of the book

Plot and Structure

Plot

Part One

Chapter 1

The reader is introduced to the Finch family of Maycomb and to the town itself. We learn the story of Boo Radley, and Dill arrives to stay. The story starts when Scout is six and Jem is ten.

- An argument between Jem and Scout about the start of events leading to Jem's broken arm takes us into the main story.
- The history and background of the family and town set the scene for what follows.
- Dill's arrival starts the game of making Boo Radley come out, which leads to Boo taking an interest in the children and vice versa.

> **Key quotations**
>
> I maintain that the Ewells started it all, but Jem, who was four years my senior, said it started long before that. He said it began the summer Dill came to us, when Dill first gave us the idea of making Boo Radley come out. *(Chapter 1)*

Writers often introduce important characters and themes in the opening chapter of a novel. Referring to this first chapter can be useful in your essay answer.

> **Activity 1**
>
> Work with a partner and make a timeline of the events in the novel like the one below, adding more events as required.
>
>
>
> **1**
> Dill's arrival and getting Boo Radley to come out

Chapters 2 and 3

Scout's first day at school is not a success. She is well ahead of the curriculum and is told that her father must not read with her. Her efforts to explain local customs and knowledge get her into further trouble. At lunchtime she is again in trouble for being rude to Walter Cunningham and by the end of the day she refuses to go back to school. Her father Atticus agrees they will continue reading if she returns to school.

- The reader is shown differences between the town families and rural families, who suffer from poverty and poor education.
- We are introduced to the Cunninghams and the Ewells, who will play a significant role in later events.
- Scout learns about the idea of compromise from Atticus, a skill she will need later in the novel.

> **Key quotations**
>
> **Miss Caroline seemed unaware that the ragged, denim-shirted and floursack-skirted first grade, most of whom had chopped cotton and fed hogs from the time they were able to walk, were immune to imaginative literature.** *(Chapter 2)*

Scout reads to Atticus in the 1962 film *To Kill a Mockingbird*

Chapters 4–7

The children find little gifts in a hole in the Radley oak tree. They are about to post a thank you letter when Nathan Radley cements in the hole, which makes Jem very upset.

Scout feels left out by Jem and Dill and spends more time with Miss Maudie Atkinson, who loves her garden and hates her house. There, Scout learns more about the Radleys.

The plans to get Boo Radley to come out continue, even after Atticus has warned them to leave him alone, culminating in a midnight attempt to peer through the windows, which leads to the children nearly being shot.

- The gifts in the tree are a sign of Boo Radley's interest in the children and the mending and return of Jem's trousers show his protective feelings towards them.
- The cementing of the oak tree reveals Nathan Radley's determination to keep the family isolated.
- Scout's friendship with Miss Maudie is important to her as she grows older and tries to understand her society.

> **Key quotations**
>
> Two live oaks stood at the edge of the Radley lot; their roots reached out into the side-road and made it bumpy. Something about one of the trees attracted my attention. *(Chapter 4)*
>
> I spent most of the remaining twilights that summer sitting with Miss Maudie Atkinson on her front porch. *(Chapter 5)*
>
> Halfway through the collards I tripped; as I tripped the roar of a shotgun shattered the neighbourhood. *(Chapter 6)*

Chapter 8

Snow falls for the first time in many years and the children build a snowman. Miss Maudie's house catches fire and is destroyed, despite the attempts of her neighbours to save it. Scout finds herself mysteriously wrapped in a blanket.

- A lighter moment in the book shows Jem as artistic and mischievous.
- We see Miss Maudie as stoical, accepting the destruction of her house without complaining.
- The townspeople are shown in a good light, risking injury to save things from the house, before we see them in a different light later in the story.
- The blanket is another hint of Boo Radley's protective attitude towards the children.

> **Key quotations**
>
> The men of Maycomb, in all degrees of dress and undress, took furniture from Miss Maudie's house to a yard across the street. *(Chapter 8)*
>
> "Boo Radley. You were so busy looking at the fire you didn't know it when he put the blanket around you." *(Chapter 8)*

Chapter 9

Scout gets into fights at school over insults to Atticus for accepting the defence of a black man. At Christmas the children receive shotguns from their father and Scout gets into a fight with her cousin Francis over his comments about Atticus.

She is beaten by her Uncle Jack but later overhears Atticus telling him that she must learn to keep control because there will be a difficult time ahead with the Ewells' accusation against Tom Robinson.

- There are several hints in this chapter of the way the townsfolk think about black people and their resentment towards Atticus for agreeing to defend Tom Robinson, which will deepen as the book goes on.
- The guns are given on condition that the children use them sensibly.
- Scout's aggression on behalf of her father shows her immaturity and he makes her promise not to defend him in that way because he knows she will have to learn about prejudice.

> **Key quotations**
>
> "Then why did Cecil say you defended niggers? He made it sound like you were runnin' a still." *(Chapter 9)*
>
> "What bothers me is that she and Jem will have to absorb some ugly things pretty soon. I'm not worried about Jem keeping his head, but Scout'd just as soon jump on someone as look at him if her pride's at stake..." *(Chapter 9)*

Chapters 10 and 11

The children are very surprised to find their peaceable and 'elderly' father is a crack shot when Heck Tate insists he shoot the rabid dog Tim Johnson. He tells them it is not courage, but the children don't believe him. When Jem, infuriated by Mrs Dubose's insults against Atticus, destroys her camellias, Atticus makes him go and read to her every afternoon. Scout loyally goes with him until they are released. When Mrs Dubose dies shortly afterwards, Atticus tells Jem that she showed real courage in overcoming her addiction to morphine in order to die as an independent person.

Atticus takes the gun to shoot the dog in the 1962 film *To Kill a Mockingbird*

- These two incidents show the children what their father's idea of courage is, which is related to what he will need in order to defend Tom Robinson and what they will need when he does so.
- The events also show the children that people are not just what they appear on the surface but have traits they keep hidden.
- It also shows the children's loyalty to each other and to Atticus, something else they will need in the coming ordeal.

Key quotations

"I think maybe he put his gun down when he realized that God had given him an unfair advantage over most living things. I guess he decided he wouldn't shoot till he had to, and he had to today." *(Chapter 10)*

"I wanted you to see what real courage is, instead of getting the idea that courage is a man with a gun in his hand." *(Chapter 11)*

Remember: Don't just retell the story of the novel in your exam – select information relevant to the question in your answer.

 Activity 2

Make a storyboard of the main events in Part One, like the one shown below. Add more sections as needed.

1. Jem condescended to take me.

2.

3.

4.

Part Two

Chapter 12

Scout is now eight. Jem is twelve and Calpurnia treats him like a man, creating a further distance between him and Scout. While Atticus is away, Calpurnia takes the children to her own church, First Purchase, on Sunday. They hear the congregation line singing hymns, led by Calpurnia's son Zeebo. Reverend Sykes takes a collection for Helen Robinson and the children find out that Tom is accused of raping Mayella Ewell.

- We are shown **segregation** in action when the children go to a black church, preparing us for what happens at the trial.
- One member of the congregation shows prejudice towards them, so we see that the prejudice is on both sides.
- Most of the congregation is welcoming – a contrast with the white community's attitude towards black people.
- The collection for Helen Robinson in the midst of great poverty shows a Christian spirit in contrast to many of the white Christian communities, as shown by the Radleys and later the Missionary tea party.
- The high stakes of the trial are revealed as the crime of rape is an offence that carries the death penalty.

> **segregation** the policy of having separate facilities for different racial groups within a society

Key quotations

"You ain't got no business bringin' white chillun here – they got their church, we got our'n. It is our church, ain't it, Miss Cal?" *(Chapter 12)*

"I want all of you with no children to make a sacrifice and give one more dime apiece. Then we'll have it." *(Chapter 12)*

"Old Mr Bob Ewell accused him of rapin' his girl an' had him arrested an' put in jail –" *(Chapter 12)*

The Church was an important element of community life for black people living in the southern states of America in the 1930s

Chapters 13 and 14

Aunt Alexandra comes to stay, to give Atticus support during the hard weeks ahead. She tries to make the children aware of the importance of family background and breeding, and sets Atticus to do the same. The children don't really understand why she wants them to behave like a lady and gentleman, and she and Atticus disagree about firing Calpurnia, whose house she forbids Scout to visit. Dill is found hiding under Scout's bed as he has run away from home.

- The **social hierarchy** of Maycomb is brought out here – it is important to Aunt Alexandra, but the children accept people for who they are.

- The growing difference between Scout and Jem is made clear by Jem's trying to make Scout do what he says because he wants his father to be less worried and by his revelation to Atticus of Dill's presence. This rational attitude will be shown as he follows the trial.

- Dill shows the importance of parental care – he has two parents who have no time for him, whereas Atticus puts his children first.

caste system a Hindu system where people are ranked by the social class they are born into; generally used to describe any class system in a society

enmity a feeling of hostility towards someone

social hierarchy a system where people are ranked in society according to status

Key quotations

There was indeed a **caste system** in Maycomb, but to my mind it worked this way: the older citizens, the present generation of people who had lived side by side for years and years, were utterly predictable to one another; they took for granted attitudes, character shadings, even gestures as having been repeated in each generation and refined by time. *(Chapter 13)*

Key quotations

I felt the starched walls of a pink cotton penitentiary closing in on me...
(Chapter 14)

"... he – they just wasn't interested in me... they stayed gone all the time, and when they were home, even, they'd get off in a room by themselves." *(Chapter 14)*

Chapter 15

On two occasions in this chapter the children see a group of men surround their father. The first group is men they know, who try to persuade Atticus to change his mind about the trial. The second is when a lynch mob arrives at the jail from out of town and threatens Atticus.

- This chapter shows another example of courage from Atticus, witnessed by his children.
- The reader is made aware of the thin veil between lawful and lawless behaviour in Maycomb. It is only later that Scout associates Atticus facing the mob with him facing Tim Johnson.
- The men are similar to those who will be on the jury at Tom's trial and we have a glimpse of their probable attitude.
- Jem's stubborn refusal to leave and Scout's naive conversation with Walter Cunningham turn the tide and show us that there is some decency even in a lynch mob.

Key quotations

Atticus said nothing. I looked around and up at Mr Cunningham, whose face was equally impassive. Then he did a peculiar thing. He squatted down and took me by both shoulders.

"I'll tell him you said hey, little lady," he said. *(Chapter 15)*

Chapters 16–20

These chapters cover the trial of Tom Robinson. The reader is shown Atticus as a defence lawyer, gradually revealing how it was impossible for Tom Robinson to have committed the crime he is charged with. From answers to Atticus's questions we see the kind of life led by Mayella Ewell, the kind of man Tom is and how he tried to help her. The children watch from the black gallery as Atticus uses his skill to show the court what really happened.

- These chapters are at the centre of the story.
- Atticus is shown to be a clever advocate as well as a caring and considerate man, although he incurs the **enmity** of Bob Ewell as a result – enmity that drives the rest of the plot.

- Jem is shown to have some legal knowledge and an ability to see what Atticus is doing, unlike Scout and Dill.
- We learn that Dill is very sensitive to mockery and injustice, and he and Scout learn about 'face-saving' from Dolphus Raymond, a lesson Scout will use later at the Missionary tea party.

Key quotations

"But you didn't call a doctor? While you were there did anyone send for one, fetch one, carry her to one?" *(Chapter 17)*

Mr Tate said, "Oh yes, that'd make it right. It was her right eye, Mr Finch. I remember now, she was bunged up on that side of her face..." *(Chapter 17)*

If her right eye was blacked and she was beaten mostly on the right side of the face, it would tend to show that a left-handed person did it. *(Chapter 17)*

"What did your father see in the window, the crime of rape or the best defence to it? Why don't you tell the truth, child? Didn't Bob Ewell beat you up?" *(Chapter 18)*

"What was the evidence of her offence? Tom Robinson, a human being. She must put Tom Robinson away from her. Tom Robinson was her daily reminder of what she did. What did she do? She tempted a Negro." *(Chapter 20)*

The children watch the trial from the public gallery in the 1962 film *To Kill a Mockingbird*

Chapters 21–23

Although a guilty verdict is inevitable, Atticus counts it as a success that the jury debated for several hours. The black community appreciate Atticus's actions and fill his kitchen with gifts of food. Jem is upset by the verdict, but Atticus says they have a good chance on appeal. When the children are disillusioned by the people of Maycomb, Miss Maudie points out that not all of them are intolerant. Bob Ewell spits at Atticus and swears revenge.

- These chapters show the depth of the prejudice in Maycomb, but also some hope of future justice.
- Aunt Alexandra upsets the children by calling the Cunninghams 'trash' and refusing to invite them in; the reader is made aware of the social snobbery as well as racial intolerance of the town.
- The children are learning about the less attractive side of the place they always felt safe in and why Boo Radley might choose to be isolated.
- Bob Ewell's action is a hint of more unpleasantness to come.

> **Key quotations**
>
> "How could they do it, how could they?"
>
> "I don't know, but they did it. They've done it before and they did it tonight and they'll do it again and when they do it – seems that only children weep." *(Chapter 22)*
>
> "I think I'm beginning to understand why Boo Radley's stayed shut up in the house all this time... it's because he *wants* to stay inside." *(Chapter 23)*

Chapters 24–26

Scout is helping Aunt Alexandra at her tea party for the local church ladies who support a mission to the Mruna tribe in Africa. Atticus arrives home unexpectedly and tells them Tom Robinson has been shot dead while trying to escape. He takes Calpurnia to break the news to Helen and meets Jem on the way. The news spreads and Bob Ewell comments about 'two to go'. Later Scout has a Current Events lesson in school, in which the teacher is shocked at Hitler's persecution of the Jews.

- Scout sees another kind of courage from her aunt and Miss Maudie as they recover from Atticus's news and carry on serving tea.
- We are shown the hypocrisy of Maycomb society as the ladies complain about their black servants' poor attitude after the trial, while supporting a mission for black people abroad.
- This hypocrisy extends even to the teachers, who discriminate against people in their town while lamenting Hitler's discriminations in Germany.

- The one bright spot is Mr Underwood's leader in the *Maycomb Tribune*, which is highly critical of Tom's shooting even though Atticus says that Mr Underwood dislikes black people.
- Bob Ewell's comment is another hint of what will happen later on.

Key quotations

"The handful of people in this town who say that fair play is not marked White Only; the handful of people who say a fair trial is for everybody, not just us; the handful of people with enough humility to think, when they look at a Negro, there but for the Lord's kindness am I... The handful of people in this town with background, that's who they are."
(Chapter 24)

"Jem, how can you hate Hitler so bad an' then turn around and be ugly about folks right at home – ?" *(Chapter 26)*

Chapters 27–31

Bob Ewell stalks Helen Robinson until Link Deas stops him. Judge Taylor's house is broken into. Scout is to play a ham in the Halloween pageant, but Atticus and her aunt give excuses for not attending. On the way to school they are frightened by Cecil Jacobs near the Radley oak. Scout misses her cue in the pageant and enters late, spoiling the finale. Later she and Jem are attacked while walking home in the dark. Someone rescues them and carries Jem home. The doctor says he will be all right, as will Scout, and Heck Tate finds Bob Ewell lying dead under the tree. Atticus thinks Jem has killed him, but Heck Tate shows him the truth. It was Boo Radley who saved the children, but to put him on trial would be cruel. Scout meets Boo at last and realizes, as she stands on the Radley porch, that Atticus was right to say you only understand someone when you see things from their point of view.

- These chapters are the final part of the story and finally tell us how Jem's arm was broken, linking us to the opening of the novel.
- Boo Radley finally comes out to protect the children he has watched from inside his house – another link to the start of the book.
- All the hints about Bob Ewell's threats finally reach fruition in his attempt to get back at Atticus by murdering his children.
- The sheriff does the decent, if not the legal, thing by insisting Bob Ewell fell on his knife in order to spare Boo Radley publicity.
- Scout imagines Boo Radley seeing things from his house and realizes that people cannot be judged by how they seem to others.

Key quotations

Mr Tate found his neck and rubbed it. "Bob Ewell's lyin' on the ground under that tree down yonder with a kitchen knife stuck up under his ribs. He's dead, Mr Finch." *(Chapter 28)*

Atticus fetched the remains of my costume. Mr Tate turned it over and bent it around to get an idea of its former shape. "This thing probably saved her life," he said. "Look."

He pointed with a long forefinger. A shiny clean line stood out on the dull wire. "Bob Ewell meant business," Mr Tate muttered. *(Chapter 29)*

Atticus looked like he needed cheering up. I ran to him and hugged him and kissed him with all my might. "Yes sir, I understand," I reassured him. "Mr Tate was right."

Atticus disengaged himself and looked at me. "What do you mean?"

"Well, it'd be sort of like shootin' a mockingbird, wouldn't it?" *(Chapter 30)*

Atticus was right. One time he said you never really know a man until you stand in his shoes and walk around in them. Just standing on the Radley porch was enough. *(Chapter 31)*

Activity 3

1. Complete a storyboard for the main events in Part Two.

2. Make a map of Maycomb, using information given in the novel. In a small group, discuss what is significant about the area where the children spend most of their time. Why does Harper Lee want to emphasize the size of Scout's world?

Structure

Time scheme

The events of the novel take place over a period of three years, starting from when Scout was six and Jem ten, and finishing when Scout was nine and Jem 13. The first paragraph of the book is about Jem getting his arm broken when he was 13. It continues, **'When enough years had gone by to enable us to look back on them, we sometimes discussed the events leading to his accident'** *(Chapter 1)*. This tells us that the novel is about things that happened in the past and that the narrator, Scout, is now grown up.

The events that happen in Part One take place over a span of two years and at the beginning of Part Two we are told **'Jem was twelve'** *(Chapter 12)*. His age is important as he is reaching puberty and Scout no longer understands him as well as she used to. He is beginning to realize things that Scout is still too young to understand and this leads to friction between them. Part Two covers one year and ends with the attack on the children when Jem's arm is broken – which takes us back to the start of the novel.

How the structure works

When writing about plot and structure in a novel, it is important for you to think about how the author uses **cause and effect**. For example, when Jem's stories about Boo Radley lead him and Dill to think of ever more elaborate schemes to get Boo to come out, resulting in the children being shot at; or when Jem's anxiety about Atticus leads to the children going to the jail and Scout dispersing the lynch mob.

You also need to consider the **narrative structure** of the novel. That is the way that the story is told by Scout, in the **first person**, but on two levels: the main **narrator** is the adult Scout, looking back to her childhood; the voice of Scout as a child comes out mainly in the **dialogue**. You need to be able to write about what the story gains from this approach in that the reader is shown what happened from a child's point of view, but with the added benefit of the adult's hindsight and vocabulary.

> **Key quotations**
>
> Atticus's remarks were still rankling which made me miss the request in Jem's question. My feathers rose again. "You tryin' to tell me what to do?" *(Chapter 14)*

cause and effect the way an action can cause something else to happen

dialogue conversation between characters in a novel

first-person narration a story told from the narrator's point of view, using the pronoun 'I'

narrative structure the way in which a writer organizes a story to create meaning

narrator the person who tells a story (Scout is the narrator in *To Kill a Mockingbird*)

protagonist the central character in a novel, around whom most of the action revolves

Activity 4

1. Part One of the novel is about the lessons the children learn. List these lessons for each child (Scout, Jem and Dill).

2. Think about the two parts of the novel. Can you come up with a subheading for each of them?

3. Harper Lee manages to show events and conversations for which Scout is not actually present in the novel (for example, by having her overhear conversations or have events reported to her by other characters). Find three examples of this.

There is also an additional point to note in that Scout is usually not considered to be the main character (**protagonist**) of the novel. This is probably Jem, because he is the one who grows up during the story, while Scout, although learning a great deal, is still only nine when it finishes. We see this process through Scout's eyes rather than her brother's and feel her bewilderment as Jem changes, as well as Jem's disillusionment with the adult world he is joining. Some critics also point to Atticus as the protagonist of the novel.

Writing about plot and structure

Upgrade

You need to know *To Kill a Mockingbird* extremely well. Although you may not be questioned directly on the plot of the novel, you need to show an understanding of the novel as a whole, including key events. This doesn't mean retelling the story; instead you should select the information that is relevant to the question.

Remember to use evidence from the text. You should have a mixture of references and direct quotations in your answer. For example, when writing about Lee's use of cause and effect, you could show how Dill's tears at the trial lead to him and Scout finding out Dolphus Raymond's secret.

Context

Biography of Harper Lee

- Nell Harper Lee was born in 1926 and grew up in Monroeville, Alabama.

- Her mother's maiden name was Finch.

- Like Atticus, her father was a local lawyer.

- Her best friend, the author Truman Capote, was the model for Dill.

- Lee studied law but gave it up to concentrate on writing.

- She wrote her only novel, *To Kill a Mockingbird,* in the 1950s and it was published in 1960, just before the black civil rights movement gained momentum.

- She was awarded the Pulitzer Prize for literature in 1961.

- In 1962, the novel was made into an Academy Award winning film, starring Gregory Peck.

- In 2007, she was given the Presidential Medal of Freedom, the highest honour that can be awarded to a civilian in the United States of America.

- Lee has avoided the limelight and refuses to give interviews. She retired to Monroeville where she still lives.

- Her book continues to be read all over the world.

Nell Harper Lee (1926–) wrote *To Kill a Mockingbird* in the 1950s and it was published in 1960

Mention the author's background *only* in relation to how it may have affected what she includes in the novel.

Historical and cultural context of the novel

There will be many things that are unfamiliar to British readers in this novel. The climate of Alabama, plants such as scuppernongs and collards, birds like bluejays and mockingbirds, the architecture of the buildings and the general way of life and of speaking may be strange to British readers. What will be familiar is human nature in all its variety, which is similar in every country and culture.

African–American rights

When Harper Lee was growing up, there was still much injustice towards black people in the southern states of America. These were the states that had a history of plantations with slave labour. They grew cotton, sugar or tobacco and they refused to recognize the rights of black people. They practised segregation in every area and **disenfranchised** black people from voting in elections. The education given to black children was virtually non-existent and they were allowed to take only the most menial jobs. Calpurnia explains line singing to the children by saying, **"Can't but about four folks in First Purchase read... I'm one of 'em"** *(Chapter 12)*. Calpurnia has a relatively high status despite being the Finch's housekeeper, because Atticus regards her as a substitute mother for the children, but Tom and Helen Robinson are field workers and Zeebo is the town's garbage collector. In every area of life at that time, black people were regarded as inferior to even the most ignorant and illiterate white person, as the trial shows. The system of segregation that regarded black people as inferior was known as '**Jim Crow**'.

disenfranchise to deprive someone of their rights of citizenship, including the right to vote

Jim Crow laws a system of racial segregation laws enacted in the United States between 1876 and 1965

Key quotations

First Purchase African M.E. Church was in the Quarters outside the southern town limits, across the old sawmill tracks. It was an ancient paint-peeled frame building, the only church in Maycomb with a steeple and bell, called First Purchase because it was paid for from the first earnings of freed slaves. Negroes worshipped in it on Sundays and white men gambled in it on weekdays. *(Chapter 12)*

In the southern states of 1930s' America, the black population lived a segregated life and usually worked in the fields or carried out other menial jobs

The trial itself has similarities to a famous trial of 1931, known as the Scottsboro Trials, where nine young black men were accused of raping two white girls on a train. Despite a lack of real evidence, they were convicted and sentenced to death. The doctor who examined the women and told the judge they had not been raped refused to testify because it would jeopardize his career. The appointed defence was inexperienced and given no time to prepare a case. The jury was all white – inevitably because Alabama had refused black voting rights and only voters could be jurors. The main prosecution witness was a white prostitute who was trying to evade prosecution herself, as her companion later testified, but insisted she had been raped throughout the trials. The prison and courthouse were surrounded by lynch mobs, and prisoners and defence lawyers had to be protected by the National Guard. Lee shows Judge Taylor to be unusually impartial and the people of Maycomb to be less aggressive than the real people of Alabama were in the Scottsboro Trials.

Key quotations

"Did it ever strike you that Judge Taylor naming Atticus to defend that boy was no accident? That Judge Taylor might have had his reasons for naming him?" *(Chapter 22)*

Remember: use your knowledge of social and historical context only as it is relevant to the exam question. Don't write a history essay!

Activity 1

Discuss and make notes on the following:

a) what we learn about the Jim Crow system from:

- the children's visit to First Purchase (Chapter 12)
- Aunt Alexandra's attitude towards Calpurnia (Chapter 13)
- the way the Maycomb ladies talk about their servants at the tea party (Chapter 24);

b) the similarities and differences between the Scottsboro Trials and the trial of Tom Robinson. Consider:

- the appearance of lynch mobs (Chapters 15 and 16)
- the all-white jury (Chapter 16)
- Mayella Ewell's insistence that she was raped by Tom Robinson, despite the lack of evidence (Chapter 18)
- the appointment of Atticus as defence lawyer by Judge Taylor (Chapter 9)
- Judge Taylor's handling of the trial (Chapters 18–22).

Modern attitudes

It is important to remember that racial and social attitudes have changed considerably since the book was written and even more so since the time in which it is set. The America of the 1930s would have considered it unthinkable to have a black president.

Students today will find themselves very uncomfortable with the use of the term 'nigger', for example, which is used frequently in the novel. They may also be unhappy about the depiction of black characters, who are mainly passive victims or at least appear to accept their inferior role in society. Remember, Harper Lee was writing as a white member of a southern community during the 1950s at the start of the **African–American civil rights movement** and the book was published before Martin Luther King made his famous speech.

African–American civil rights movement a political movement in the United States (1955–1968) aimed at outlawing racial discrimination and giving voting and other civil rights to black citizens

Participants carry the American flag on the black civil rights march from Selma to Montgomery, Alabama in 1965

Activity 2

Work in a small group to research the history of the black civil rights movement in America. You should begin with American involvement in the slave trade from the early 18th century and trace the progress of black freedom and rights down to the election of President Obama. You should also include the activities of lynch mobs and the Ku Klux Klan.

Put your findings and suitable pictures on a large sheet of paper for display in your classroom.

The Great Depression

The **Wall Street crash** occured in 1929 and was followed by years of widespread poverty and unemployment across the USA. Farmers were hit particularly hard and, as the southern states were mainly agricultural, this had a knock-on effect throughout their societies. Even plantation owners like Link Deas felt the pinch, having to lay off workers, who were mainly black, while small farmers like Walter Cunningham were often reduced to accepting parish handouts in order to survive, or paying for services with what they could grow.

> **Wall Street crash** a devastating stock market crash in 1929 which signalled the beginning of the Great Depression

Key quotations

Atticus said professional people were poor because the farmers were poor. As Maycomb County was farm country, nickels and dimes were hard to come by for doctors and dentists and lawyers. *(Chapter 2)*

Disastrous farming conditions and harvests, caused by severe drought and over-farming, added to the poverty of 1930s' America

American Civil War

Although the book is set many years after the civil war, its effects and attitudes can still be seen in Maycomb. The war started in 1861 when the southern states created a Confederacy to break away from the United States of America. They did this because of the election of Abraham Lincoln, who was strongly opposed to slavery. After four years of savage fighting, the Union won and slavery was officially ended. However, it left the Confederate states feeling bitter about the loss of their revenues and with their racist outlook unchanged. Mrs Dubose is an example of the bigoted attitudes held by many and was believed to have an old CSA (Confederate States of America) pistol with her at all times.

> **Key quotations**
>
> Simon [Finch] would have regarded with impotent fury the disturbance between the North and the South, as it left his descendants stripped of everything but their land... *(Chapter 1)*
>
> Cousin Ike Finch was Maycomb County's sole surviving Confederate veteran... Jem and I would listen respectfully to Atticus and Cousin Ike rehash the war. *(Chapter 9)*

> **Activity 3**
>
> Work with a partner or in a small group to make a PowerPoint presentation of the causes, events and aftermath of the American Civil War.
>
> You should select the most important episodes and find pictures to illustrate your presentation, along with captions and your own notes. Wherever possible, you should try and refer to the novel or use quotations from it.
>
> You could use suitable music to accompany your presentation, such as:
>
> - *John Brown's Body* (Union)
> - *Marching Through Georgia* (Union)
> - *Dixie's Land* (Confederate)
> - *When Johnny Comes Marching Home* (Confederate)
>
> All of these and some others can be found online.

Culture and attitudes

Many people in the southern states were descended from English or French settlers who had bought land as an investment or who had left Europe because of religious persecution, like the Finch ancestor who was a Methodist in Cornwall. As Scout comments 'Being Southerners, it was a source of shame to some members of the family that we had no recorded ancestors on either side of the Battle of Hastings' *(Chapter 1)*. Their Christian religion did not apparently prevent them from owning slaves, as Simon Finch's plantation at Finch's Landing showed. Like many others, the Finch family were left with only their land after the Civil War. The snobbery of these old families remained and is the reason for Aunt Alexandra's insistence that the children remember their background and behave like 'a gentleman' and 'a lady'. Most of Maycomb's population are Baptists, Methodists or Presbyterians by religion.

There is a definite social hierarchy in Maycomb, which has the 'old' families and professional people like the Finches and Miss Maudie Atkinson at the top, followed by trades people and 'respectable' families; the small farmers, such as the Cunninghams, are low down the scale and 'white trash' like the Ewells are at the bottom. Below all of these is the black community, which is not even considered to be part of the social fabric and lives in a separate area out of town. Even the most enlightened whites have this attitude to some extent.

> **Key quotations**
>
> There was indeed a caste system in Maycomb, but to my mind it worked this way: the older citizens, the present generation of people who had lived side by side for years and years, were utterly predictable to one another; they took for granted attitudes, character shadings, even gestures, as having been repeated in each generation and refined by time. *(Chapter 13)*

This scene from the 1962 film shows a cross-section of Maycomb white society; the black community had to watch from the gallery

Maycomb has typical small-town attitudes. Most of the residents are related to each other and family traits are known to all. As Jem says, referring to his aunt's gossip, "Aunty better watch how she talks – scratch most folks in Maycomb and they're kin to us" *(Chapter 13)*. The inhabitants are not particularly interested in happenings outside the county. As Scout tells us, probably repeating what she has heard, 'North Alabama was full of Liquor Interests, Big Mules, steel companies, Republicans, professors, and other persons of no background' *(Chapter 2)*. Few people leave Maycomb and even fewer move into it, so the population is static and this means that everyone knows everyone else.

Most of the townsfolk love gossiping – there is not much else to do and when every phone call is routed through an operator who knows everyone, there is little that remains private for long. This is why a dramatic event such as the trial of Tom Robinson creates such a stir: 'It was like Saturday. People from the south end of the county passed our house in a leisurely but steady stream' *(Chapter 16)*.

They are also hypocritical; this is shown at the Missionary tea party where the Maycomb ladies gather to raise funds for the Mruna tribe of Africa, while complaining about the poor attitude of their own black servants following the trial. It puzzles Scout when she remembers overhearing her teacher, who had been indignant about Hitler's treatment of the Jews, commenting after the trial: "… it's time somebody taught 'em a lesson, they were gettin' way above themselves, an' the next thing they think they can do is marry us" *(Chapter 26)*. She asks Jem, "how can you hate Hitler so bad an' then turn around and be ugly about folks right at home – ?" *(Chapter 26)*.

Key quotations

Maycomb was an old town, but it was a tired old town when I first knew it. In rainy weather the streets turned to red slop; grass grew on the sidewalks, the courthouse sagged in the square. Somehow, it was hotter then; a black dog suffered on a summer's day; bony mules hitched to Hoover carts flicked flies in the sweltering shade of the live oaks on the square. Men's stiff collars wilted by nine in the morning. Ladies bathed before noon, after their three o'clock naps, and by nightfall were like soft teacakes with frostings of sweat and sweet talcum.

People moved slowly then. They ambled across the square, shuffled in and out of the stores around it, took their time about everything. A day was twenty-four hours long but seemed longer. There was no hurry, for there was nowhere to go, nothing to buy and no money to buy it with, nothing to see outside the boundaries of Maycomb County. *(Chapter 1)*

Activity 4

1. Using the description of Maycomb on page 27 and your knowledge of the rest of the book, write an entry about the town for a 1935 travel guide to Alabama.

2. Imagine you were a visitor to Maycomb in the 1930s. Write a letter to a friend or relation giving your impressions of the town and its inhabitants.

Books and superstitions

The children are constantly reading and have their favourite stories, which they act out in the yard. Their favourites are *Tarzan*, *The Rover Boys* and *Tom Swift*. They like tales of ghosts and 'haints' and Hot Steams, which **"go around at night suckin' people's breath –"** *(Chapter 4)* according to Jem. Dill's retelling of the film *Dracula* is a hit with children living in a town with no cinema.

Most of the superstitious stories concern Boo Radley, including the one that the pecans that fall from the Radley tree into the schoolyard are poisoned. Boo Radley himself is said to prowl around at night and Miss Stephanie Crawford provokes a sharp retort from Miss Maudie when she claims to have seen him peering in at her window. These **gothic** stories appeal to the children, who make up their own games about Boo Radley. In these games the children are partly acting out the grown-up world of violence and prejudice and partly trying to make sense of their own fears.

> **gothic** a literary style characterized by tales of horror and the supernatural

Activity 5

Working with a partner, look at the description of the Radley place and the stories about Boo Radley in Chapter 1. Then use a search engine or an encyclopaedia to find out more about gothic literature. Discuss and make notes about how you think ideas of the gothic can be applied to Harper Lee's portrayal of the Radley house and family.

Writing about context

Upgrade

You may need to relate *To Kill a Mockingbird* to its social, cultural and historical context and to explain how the text has been influential to readers at different times.

To gain the marks awarded for this area, you need to relate the question to the background and setting of *To Kill a Mockingbird*. This does not mean that you should write all you know about it! It does mean that you should show how an understanding of the part of the novel you are writing about benefits from knowing something about the time in which it was written.

For example, if you are asked a question about (or involving) Bob Ewell, it would be difficult to answer fully without mentioning that he embodies all the worst of the racial prejudice in similar towns at the time and that the Great Depression made things significantly worse for families such as the Ewells.

You could also mention how readers in the 1960s might have understood the book, when the Civil Rights movement was beginning to gain real momentum. They might well have seen this novel as a rather daring call to support the black Americans who were demanding equal treatment with whites.

As modern readers, we have the benefit of hindsight and so the way we read the book is very different. Although racism unfortunately continues to be a part of some people's thinking, it is no longer condoned by any public body and there are laws prohibiting anyone from inciting racial hatred. That makes it more difficult for us to understand the attitudes of people in the novel, but it should also help us to realize how those like Atticus Finch were beacons of justice and humanity in a dark world.

Main characters

Scout

Scout's proper name is Jean Louise Finch and she is the narrator of the story, which covers events in her life between the ages of six and nine. She lives in Maycomb with her father Atticus, a lawyer, and her older brother Jem, but the reader sees things through her eyes, both at the time they are happening and as she looks back on them when she is an adult.

Scout is a tomboy who enjoys the freedom of wearing overalls and gets into fights with the boys at school. Her reaction to a problem is to use her fists. When she gets into trouble with Miss Caroline for standing up for Walter Cunningham, she beats him up in the schoolyard. When Dill, having asked her to marry him, then forgets about her, she says, **'I beat him up twice but it did no good, he only grew closer to Jem'** *(Chapter 5).* This aggressive approach doesn't seem to solve things, as she comes to realize.

One of the lessons she learns from Atticus is that violence is not the answer. He makes her promise not to fight over any insults she hears about him. So when Cecil Jacobs insults Atticus, Scout remembers her promise and walks away, feeling noble that she has been called a coward for Atticus. Although she doesn't understand why people are insulting her father, she will do what she can to defend him. She does this through her innocent questioning of Mr Walter Cunningham, which makes the lynch mob aware of what they are doing.

Scout isn't interested in the things that Aunt Alexandra thinks she should be doing, like wearing dresses and playing with dolls. She sees those as limiting her freedom and she feels uncomfortable in the company of women. Scout has a trying time with her aunt, who wants to turn her into a 'lady': **'My heart sank... I felt the starched walls of a pink cotton penitentiary closing in on me, and for the second time in my life I thought of running away'** *(Chapter 4).* However, later on, when they learn about Tom Robinson's death, Scout realizes there is more to being a lady, as she watches her aunt put on a brave face and carry on with the tea party: **'After all, if Aunty could be a lady at a time like this, so could I'** *(Chapter 24).* Her main role models early on are Calpurnia and Miss Maudie Atkinson, both of whom are strong, independent women with high standards. Calpurnia is very strict with Scout and teaches her good manners and consideration for others. When Scout comments on Walter Cunningham's table manners, Calpurnia gives her a slap and makes her eat in the kitchen. Miss Maudie talks to Scout about the Radleys and tells her the way things really are. She stands up for Scout at the Missionary tea party and it is through her that Scout realizes Aunt Alexandra is human after all.

Scout is frightened of Boo Radley – more so than Jem or Dill. She tries to persuade them to stop playing games based on him after she hears laughter coming from the Radley house when she spills from the tyre. She fearfully imagines him prowling round the house.

Scout talks to Boo in the 1962 film *To Kill a Mockingbird*

It is only after the really terrible events surrounding the trial, that Scout realizes Boo Radley is not to be feared. There is more real evil to be found among people she had always felt safe with. Part of her **coming of age** is to see things differently and to realize the **irony** that when Boo Radley finally did come out it was to save her and Jem from being murdered. When she finally sees him in the flesh, she understands he is a shy, gentle man and feels sad that she and Jem have given him nothing in return for all he has given them. As she sees things from his house she reflects, '**Atticus was right. One time he said you never really know a man until you stand in his shoes and walk around in them. Just standing on the Radley porch was enough'** *(Chapter 31).*

Scout is made aware of the hypocrisy of many of Maycomb's inhabitants when she helps out at Aunt Alexandra's tea party; here, she listens to the ladies, who claim to be devout Christians raising money for Africans, complain about their underpaid servants. She also questions why her teacher is indignant about Hitler's persecution of the Jews, after making racist comments following the trial.

Her **naivety** creates much of the book's humour, as she sees things from the perspective of a child; for example, '**Atticus was feeble: he was nearly fifty'** *(Chapter 10)* or '**the town council told Mr Radley that if he didn't take Boo back, Boo would die of mould from the damp'** *(Chapter 1).*

> **coming of age** growing into adulthood through knowledge and experience
>
> **irony** the discrepancy between what a character could be expected to do and what they actually do, often for comic effect
>
> **naivety** innocence

 Activity 1

Scout's coming of age in the novel is more subtle than Jem's.

a) With a partner, discuss the following:

- Scout's attitude to Boo Radley at the beginning and end of the book
- Scout's view about being 'a lady' at the start of the book and after the tea party
- Scout's feelings for Jem at the beginning, after the trial and at the end
- Scout's attitude to violence at the beginning and end of the book.

b) Find evidence in the book to support your ideas.

c) Write a brief account of the changes in Scout, covering the three years of the novel, from Miss Maudie's point of view.

Jem

Jem's full name is Jeremy Atticus Finch and he is the only son of Atticus and older brother of Scout. Jem grows from ten to 13 years of age during the course of the story and we are shown the changes in him as he grows up, through Scout's eyes. Scout doesn't understand why Jem is changing as he grows older, but Calpurnia does, when she begins to call him 'Mister Jem'.

Jem is a thoughtful boy who thinks about things logically, but is also very sensitive to others. That is why he cries when he finds that the knot hole in the oak tree has been cemented, because he understands that Nathan Radley has done it to prevent Boo communicating with him and Scout. He tries to look after Scout and is fond of her in his own way. When he finds her chewing gum she found in the Radley oak, he tells her off: "Don't you know you're not supposed to even touch the trees over there? You'll get killed if you do!" *(Chapter 4)* and he makes her gargle, just in case. He respects his father and is usually careful not to do anything he thinks might annoy or upset him. He is delighted when Atticus praises him over the Mr Avery snowman and tries to persuade Scout not to rile Aunt Alexandra because he knows it makes things more difficult for his father. After Atticus shoots the rabid dog and Scout wants to tell everyone, Jem tells her not to, saying, "Naw, Scout, it's something you wouldn't understand. Atticus is real old, but I wouldn't care if he couldn't do anything – I wouldn't care if he couldn't do a blessed thing... Atticus is a gentleman, just like me!" *(Chapter 10)*.

Jem is a footballer (American style) and his ambition is to play for his school. He has a vivid imagination fed by the books he reads, as we see when he makes up games based on them. He also enjoys making up stories about Boo Radley and he and Dill try to think of ways to get Boo Radley to come out. These come to an abrupt end after the children are nearly shot by Nathan Radley and when Jem finds his trousers, badly mended, on the fence. He has understood that Boo Radley was trying to protect him, which is why he spills everything out to Atticus when Scout finds the blanket round her shoulders after the fire at Miss Maudie's.

Unlike his younger sister, Jem is very well aware of why the other children are shouting insults about their father. He finds the whole affair of the trial more troubling than Scout and the incident with Mrs Dubose's camellias happens because she called their father names. Jem learns to control his anger and let the insults wash over him, but he becomes rather silent, moody and distant from Scout, who tries to make allowances.

It is Jem who realizes that Atticus may be in danger. He creates a diversion when a group of men seem to be threatening his father on their porch and he decides to visit Atticus outside the town prison when the lynch mob arrives. He defies Atticus, when his father orders him home, and Scout sees how alike they are when their honour and conscience are involved.

During the trial, Jem follows his father's cross-examinations with interest and can understand what Atticus is doing. This makes him confident that Tom Robinson is innocent and that therefore the jury must acquit him. He is devastated when the verdict comes in and his faith in Maycomb is destroyed. He asks his father, "How could they do it, how could they?" *(Chapter 22)*. He tells Miss Maudie, "It's like bein' a caterpillar in a cocoon... Like somethin' asleep wrapped up in a warm place. I always thought Maycomb folks were the best folks in the world, least that's what they seemed like" *(Chapter 22)*.

Jem is brave and this is part of his code of honour. He is afraid of the Radley place and therefore accepts Dill's dare to touch it, and he returns for his missing trousers because he would rather risk being shot by Nathan Radley than face Atticus's disappointment in him. As he grows up, he passes on his increasing knowledge to Scout, although she doesn't really appreciate the superior way in which he does it.

Later, when Scout says there's 'only one kind of folks', he tells her, "That's what I thought, too... when I was your age. If there's just one kind of folks, why can't they get along with each other? If they're all alike, why do they go out of their way to despise each other?" *(Chapter 23)*.

He is also understanding when Aunt Alexandra refuses to let Scout play with Walter Cunningham and says, "You're enough of a problem to your father as it is" *(Chapter 23)*. He stops Scout doing something she would regret, 'He caught me by the shoulders, put his arm around me, and led me sobbing in fury to his bedroom' *(Chapter 23)*. He gives her a consoling wad of gum and tells Atticus, "'s not anything" *(Chapter 23)*.

He also tries to defend Scout when they are attacked by Bob Ewell at the end of the novel, badly breaking his arm in the process. At the end of the book, Jem is unconscious so only Scout meets Boo Radley and realizes his true nature.

Activity 2

Imagine you are Jem. Write your diary entries for the following:

- the incident with Tim Johnson (Chapter 10)
- the episode with Mrs Dubose (Chapter 11)
- the confrontation with the lynch mob (Chapter 15)
- the end of the trial (Chapter 22)
- the night of the school pageant (Chapter 28).

Remember to base your writing on evidence from the book. You should write in diary form, using abbreviations and informal language where appropriate.

Memorize a few short key quotations before the exam to support your points about characters.

Atticus Finch

Father of Scout and Jem, brother to Alexandra and Jack, and known by everyone in Maycomb, Atticus is the town's conscience, a difficult and sometimes dangerous role. As Miss Maudie says, *"We're so rarely called on to be Christians, but when we are, we've got men like Atticus to go for us" (Chapter 22)*.

Atticus is a single father, a role he carries out to the best of his ability by being strict but totally honest with his children, who call him by his name. He is older than most fathers with children of their ages, but he plays football with Jem, reads with Scout and tries to teach his children to be respectful and tolerant towards others. He trusts Calpurnia and always backs her up because she acts like a mother to Scout and Jem. He also uses his judicial ideas of fairness in dealing with them, always listening to both sides before he makes a judgment. Scout tells Uncle Jack, *"When Jem an' I fuss Atticus doesn't ever just listen to Jem's side of it, he hears mine too..." (Chapter 9)*.

Atticus could be considered to be the moral centre of the novel. He doesn't just tell his children how to behave, he shows them. As Miss Maudie tells Scout, *"Atticus Finch is the same in his house as he is on the public streets" (Chapter 5)*. He is courteous towards everyone, even Mrs Dubose, who calls him names and insults him, telling Scout *"... baby, it's never an insult to be called what somebody thinks is a bad name. It just shows you how poor that person is, it doesn't hurt you" (Chapter 11)*. He agrees to defend Tom Robinson because he feels it is the right thing to do, even though he knows it will make his family a target for abuse and put himself in danger. The only time he shows fear is when the children run up against the lynch mob and then it is fear for them, not himself.

As a lawyer, Atticus upholds the highest standards. When he defends Tom Robinson, he shows in open court that Tom is innocent. Atticus feels that he is not only defending Tom Robinson or the rights of black citizens in the trial, but the whole idea of American justice. He concludes his summing up with the following words to the jury:

> **Key quotations**
>
> "I'm no idealist to believe firmly in the integrity of our courts and in the jury system – that is no ideal to me, it is a living, working reality. Gentlemen, a court is no better than each man of you sitting before me on this jury. A court is only as sound as its jury, and a jury is only as sound as the men who make it up. I am confident that you gentlemen will review without passion the evidence you have heard, come to a decision, and restore this defendant to his family. In the name of God, do your duty." *(Chapter 20)*

He knows they will not do their duty but, not only does he do his very best for Tom, he treats all the witnesses with courtesy, including the lying Ewells. In contrast, the prosecuting counsel's treatment of Tom Robinson makes Dill cry.

It is also Atticus who teaches his children the meaning of true courage. They are very impressed when he shoots the mad dog cleanly with a single shot, in spite of being nearly blind in one eye. They find it hard to understand why they didn't know about his skill. Later Atticus tells Jem, "I wanted you to see what real courage is, instead of getting the idea that courage is a man with a gun in his hand. It's when you know you're licked before you begin but you begin anyway and you see it through no matter what" *(Chapter 11)*. This is exactly what Atticus himself does by agreeing to defend Tom Robinson, knowing the jury would convict him whatever the evidence said and knowing that most of the town would be against him. He counts it as a small victory that the jury takes several hours to reach its inevitable conclusion and that he did manage to convince one juror to argue for acquittal.

Scout sums it up by realizing, 'Atticus had used every tool available to free men to save Tom Robinson, but in the secret courts of men's hearts Atticus had no case. Tom was a dead man the minute Mayella Ewell opened her mouth and screamed' *(Chapter 25)*.

Atticus and Scout in the 1962 film
To Kill a Mockingbird

In spite of what happens around the trial and the spite – even evil – that this event arouses, Atticus is still able to keep his faith in human nature. At the end of the book when Scout says that Boo Radley was 'real nice', he says "Most people are, Scout, when you finally see them" *(Chapter 31)*.

Activity 3

Work with a partner to write an interview about the events outside Maycomb Jail on the night before Tom Robinson's trial. One of you should be in role as Atticus and the other should be a reporter for a local newspaper.

The reporter's questions should not be just about what happened, but about how Atticus felt about the incident, the mood of the men from Old Sarum and about the children's intervention. Remember to base your account on what is written in the novel and your own judgement of the characters. Write up your agreed version of the interview in suitable journalistic style.

Calpurnia

Key quotations

She was all angles and bones; she was nearsighted; she squinted; her hand was as wide as a bed slat and twice as hard. She was always ordering me out of the kitchen, asking me why I couldn't behave as well as Jem when she knew he was older, and calling me home when I wasn't ready to come. Our battles were epic and one-sided. Calpurnia always won, mainly because Atticus always took her side. She had been with us ever since Jem was born, and I had felt her tyrannical presence as long as I could remember. *(Chapter 1)*

Calpurnia is the Finch housekeeper. She stands in place of a mother to the children and has high expectations of them. She is not averse to giving them a smack when she thinks they deserve it, but she also comforts them and gives them treats. She protects the children from the mad dog and takes sensible action to protect others as well.

She is well-educated for a black person at the time. She can read, taught her son Zeebo to read and taught Scout to write, which causes trouble with Miss Caroline Fisher. Scout notes that, 'Atticus said Calpurnia had more education than most coloured folks' *(Chapter 3)*. She rarely comments about white people so Scout is surprised to hear her say, "There goes the meanest man ever God blew breath into" *(Chapter 1)* as she watches Mr Nathan Radley's funeral procession.

When she takes the children to First Purchase Church, Scout is stunned to find that Calpurnia leads 'a double life', having a home and family of her own and being able to speak 'two languages', but she explains by saying, "Suppose you and Scout talked coloured-folks' talk at home – it'd be out of place, wouldn't it? Now what if I talked white-folks' talk at church and with my neighbours? They'd think I was puttin' on airs to beat Moses" *(Chapter 12)*.

The relationship between Calpurnia and the Finch family is much closer than that between most Maycomb families and their black servants. Atticus is quite happy for Calpurnia to take the children to her church and for Scout to go to her house, although this is forbidden by Aunt Alexandra. Calpurnia is a cause of friction between Atticus and Aunt Alexandra, who tries to make Atticus get rid of her. It is the children's presence at the trial that unites Calpurnia and Aunt Alexandra in disapproval and they find further unity during the events of the Missionary tea party.

Aunt Alexandra

Key quotations

She was not fat, but solid, and she chose protective garments that drew up her bosom to giddy heights, pinched in her waist, flared out her rear, and managed to suggest that Aunt Alexandra's was once an hour-glass figure. From any angle it was formidable. *(Chapter 13)*

Aunt Alexandra is Atticus's sister but she is very unlike either Atticus or Uncle Jack, and is the only Finch to stay at the ancestral home at Finch's Landing. Scout thinks she could be a changeling and compares her to Mount Everest, 'she was cold and there' *(Chapter 9)*.

The children are not happy when she comes to stay with them, but the townsfolk are. She fits in straight away, becoming part of the ladies' various circles and a noted hostess. Aunt Alexandra is a gossip and a snob. She tries to instil what she calls 'good breeding' into the children, who don't understand her. She knows all the families in the area and their reputations, 'Everybody in Maycomb, it seemed, had a Streak: a Drinking Streak, a Gambling Streak, a Mean Streak, a Funny Streak' *(Chapter 13)*.

She is always nagging Scout to behave like a lady and disapproves of her clothes and behaviour. 'Aunt Alexandra's vision of my deportment involved playing with small stoves, tea sets and wearing the Add-A-Pearl necklace she gave me when I was born' *(Chapter 9)*. She also disapproves of Atticus as a father and as the defender of Tom Robinson. She is horrified to hear that the children have been to First Purchase Church and forbids Scout to visit Calpurnia. She and Atticus disagree strongly about Calpurnia, but Atticus puts his foot down and refuses to let her go.

It is the Missionary tea party, when Miss Maudie puts a stop to the malicious gossip about Atticus creating dissatisfaction among their black servants, that gives Scout a different view of her aunt: 'She gave Miss Maudie a look of pure gratitude, and I wondered at the world of women. Miss Maudie and Aunt Alexandra had never been especially close, and here was Aunty silently thanking her for something' *(Chapter 24)*. By the end of the tea party scene, Scout reflects, 'After all, if Aunty could be lady at a time like this, so could I' *(Chapter 24)*.

Aunt Alexandra is seen as progressively more human as the novel continues and by the end she is calling Scout 'darling' and patting her, showing her concern for the children after the attack.

Miss Maudie Atkinson

Miss Maudie lives opposite the Finches. She loves her garden and spends most of her time making it beautiful. The children are allowed to play in it as long as they avoid her arbour.

> **Key quotations**
>
> Miss Maudie hated her house: time spent indoors was time wasted. She was a widow, a chameleon lady who worked in her flower beds in an old straw hat and men's coveralls, but after her five o'clock bath she would appear on the porch and reign over the street in magisterial beauty. *(Chapter 5)*

Scout gets to know Miss Maudie when Jem and Dill begin leaving her out of their games. The children also discover she is an excellent cake baker. Whenever she bakes, she makes a big cake and also three small ones for the children to eat.

Miss Maudie also teaches the children what is important and what is not.

> **Key quotations**
>
> True enough she had an acid tongue in her head, and she did not go about the neighbourhood doing good, as did Miss Stephanie Crawford. But while no one with a grain of sense trusted Miss Stephanie, Jem and I had considerable faith in Miss Maudie. She had never told on us, had never played cat-and-mouse with us, she was not at all interested in our private lives. She was our friend. *(Chapter 5)*

When Miss Maudie's house burns down, she takes it in her stride, telling the children "Always wanted a smaller house, Jem Finch. Gives me more yard. Just think, I'll have more room for my azaleas now!" *(Chapter 8)*.

Miss Maudie often makes sense of various events and statements for the children. In Chapter 10, it is she who explains Atticus's rule that "it's a sin to kill a mockingbird" by telling them, "Mockingbirds don't do one thing but make music for us to enjoy. They don't eat up people's gardens, don't nest in corncribs, they don't do one thing but sing their hearts out for us. That's why it's a sin to kill a mockingbird".

After the trial, when Jem is disillusioned and asks who did anything to help Tom Robinson, she tells him, "His coloured friends for one thing, and people like us. People like Judge Taylor. People like Mr Heck Tate. Stop eating and start thinking, Jem. Did it ever strike you that Judge Taylor naming Atticus to defend that boy was no accident? That Judge Taylor might have had his reasons for naming him?" *(Chapter 22)*.

She helps Alexandra and Scout pull themselves together after the news of Tom's death by saying that 'they' are paying Atticus the tribute of trusting him to do right. When asked who 'they' are she replies, "The handful of people in this town who say that fair play is not marked White Only; the handful of people who say a fair trial is for everybody, not just us; the handful of people with enough humility to think, when they look at a Negro, there but for the Lord's kindness am I... The handful of people in this town with background, that's who they are" *(Chapter 24)*.

Dill

Dill's proper name is Charles Baker Harris and he is the nephew of Miss Rachel Haverford, the Finches' next-door neighbour.

> **Key quotations**
>
> Dill was a curiosity. He wore blue linen shorts that buttoned to his shirt, his hair was snow white and stuck to his head like duckfluff; he was a year my senior but I towered over him. As he told us the old tale his blue eyes would lighten and darken; his laugh was sudden and happy; he habitually pulled at a cowlick in the centre of his forehead. *(Chapter 1)*

Dill has a vivid imagination and it is caught up by the story of Boo Radley. He is the one who urges Jem to get Boo to come out. His father has left and, according to Aunt Alexandra, Dill is seen as a liability to his family and is passed from one member to another. He asks Scout to marry him, but then ignores her, even when she beats him up, in favour of playing and plotting with Jem. He is very quick-witted, telling the crowd gathered outside the Radley place after the shot that the children had been playing strip poker.

Dill is also a sensitive child who can't bear to see anyone getting hurt. He even gets upset when Jem talks about lighting matches under a turtle to make it come out. He makes up stories that the children do not believe.

When his mother remarries and he is no longer sent to Maycomb, Dill runs away and Scout finds him under her bed. He tells her that his mother and stepfather give him all the material things he needs, but they don't want him there; he is in the way.

When the children disturb the lynch mob, Dill plays no part in what happens, but he shows his respect for Atticus later by asking to carry his chair. At the trial he becomes very upset by the way Mr Gilmer treats Tom Robinson, calling him 'boy' and playing to the jury. Jem sends Dill out with Scout and it is he who discovers Dolphus Raymond's secret – that all he drinks is Coca-Cola – and that he is a kindred spirit who understands why Dill was crying: "Cry about the simple hell people give other people – without even thinking. Cry about the hell white people give coloured folks, without even stopping to think that they're people, too" *(Chapter 20)*.

> **Activity 4**
>
> Imagine you are Dill. Write a letter to your mother after your first few days of holiday in Maycomb. Include your thoughts and feelings about the Finch family and about Boo Radley. Use Dill's voice as much as possible and think about how he likes to tell tall stories.

Boo Radley

Boo's proper name is Arthur Radley but his nickname suggests the bogeyman he has become in the children's minds at the start of the novel. Because he never appears in public, there are all kinds of legends and stories about him. To the children, he is a frightening presence said to roam the town after dark, eating cats and squirrels, and believed to be insane.

His real story is less dramatic and very sad. After getting in with a crowd of boys who went a little too far with their teenage mischief, he was locked in the house by his father and not seen again for many years. This excessive punishment led him to stab his father in the leg with some scissors, which resulted in him being locked in the courthouse basement. His father refused to charge him and also refused to let him have treatment for mental illness, so Boo returned home.

Key quotations

Nobody knew what form of intimidation Mr Radley employed to keep Boo out of sight, but Jem figured that Mr Radley kept him chained to the bed most of the time. Atticus said no, it wasn't that sort of thing, that there were other ways of making people into ghosts. *(Chapter 1)*

When his father died, there was no relief for Boo, as his older brother Nathan immediately took his father's place. His mother was seen almost as rarely as Boo himself. The children's curiosity results in them making up stories about Boo and trying to get him to come out, which nearly gets them killed when Nathan Radley fires his shotgun at them.

Boo's relationship with the children is shown through his little acts of kindness. He puts a blanket round Scout when Miss Maudie's house is burning; he leaves little gifts for them in a knothole in one of the oaks; he tries to mend Jem's trousers when they are left behind in the children's flight from the house. Jem understands the true meanness of spirit of Nathan Radley, when he finds the knothole cemented up.

Boo's most important act is to save the children from Bob Ewell at the end of the book. When Scout finally sees him, she realizes that he is just a shy, lonely man who took comfort from observing the children.

Key quotations

His face was as white as his hands, but for a shadow on his jutting chin. His cheeks were thin to hollowness; his mouth was wide; there were shallow, almost delicate indentations at his temples, and his grey eyes were so colourless I thought he was blind. His hair was dead and thin, almost feathery on top of his head. *(Chapter 29)*

Scout is quick to understand why Heck Tate wants it to be known that Bob Ewell fell on his knife, telling Atticus, "Well, it'd be sort of like shootin' a mockingbird, wouldn't it?" *(Chapter 30)*.

Tom Robinson

Tom was a black-velvet Negro, not shiny, but soft black velvet. The whites of his eyes shone in his face, and when he spoke we saw flashes of his teeth. If he had been whole, he would have been a fine specimen of a man. *(Chapter 19)*

Tom works for Mr Link Deas, is married to Helen and is the father of several children. He is honest, hard-working and kind-hearted, which leads him into trouble. He often helps Mayella Ewell because he sees she is left alone to look after all the children and the house.

When Mayella decides to try and kiss him, Tom is terrified, knowing the impossible situation she has put him in. When her father accuses him of raping Mayella, he knows that he will face the death penalty and be tried by an all-white jury that will never take his word.

Tom is the character at the centre of the novel in many ways, as it is defending him that creates much of the hatred and abuse that the children have to learn how to deal with. It is Tom for whom the lynch mob comes, when Atticus places himself outside Maycomb Jail. It is Atticus's defence of Tom that brings insults from Mrs Dubose and which makes Jem question everything he has believed about Maycomb.

Tom Robinson on trial in the 1962 film *To Kill a Mockingbird*

Tom has to rely on Atticus to defend him and Atticus himself is the target of anger and abuse by the people of Maycomb because of this. When Tom gives evidence in court, it is clear that he could not be guilty as his left hand is useless, having been caught in a machine when he was very young. Having shown the court that Bob Ewell was the most likely abuser of his daughter and that Mayella was definitely lying, Atticus draws the true story from Tom on the witness stand.

Tom is convicted, although at least one juror argues for his acquittal, which is a kind of victory. Atticus says he will appeal and Tom is taken to the prison. Despite Atticus's assurances that they would stand a chance of overturning the verdict on appeal, Tom has seen enough of white justice and tries to escape. The guards shoot him seventeen times, which Atticus says is excessive.

Tom is one of the mockingbird characters in the novel and he is often seen as playing a passive role, depending on Atticus to fight for him; however, it is difficult to see how he could do much else in the situation.

Bob Ewell

Bob Ewell is Tom's accuser. The Ewell family are introduced with the following:

> **Key quotations**
>
> Atticus said the Ewells had been the disgrace of Maycomb for three generations. None of them had done an honest day's work in his recollection... They were people, but they lived like animals... In certain circumstances the common folk judiciously allowed them certain privileges by the simple method of becoming blind to some of the Ewells' activities. They didn't have to go to school, for one thing. Another thing, Mr Bob Ewell... was permitted to hunt and trap out of season. *(Chapter 3)*

When he is called as a witness in court, we discover that Bob Ewell is ironically named after the confederate general, Robert E. Lee. He is described as 'a little bantam cock of a man' *(Chapter 17)* and treats the courtroom as if it was the local pub, playing to the audience until Judge Taylor puts his foot down. Atticus uses cross-questioning to establish that Bob Ewell is left-handed and that he did not send for a doctor for Mayella. The evidence indicates that Bob Ewell beat up his daughter and, according to Tom Robinson's evidence that Mayella told him, "what her papa do to her don't count" *(Chapter 19)*, may have been sexually abusing her.

Although Tom is finally convicted, Bob Ewell is not satisfied. He spits in Atticus's face and tells him he will get even with him. Atticus knows that Bob fancied that he would be some sort of hero after the trial but that, in fact, the town despises him as much as ever. Atticus thinks he will be content with threats, but, as Aunt Alexandra predicts, he bears a grudge.

Bob Ewell shows his low nature by: stalking Helen Robinson, until he is frightened off by Link Deas; attempting to break into Judge Taylor's house when he thinks it is empty; and, worst of all, going after Atticus's children rather than Atticus himself. The slash of his switchblade is clear on Scout's costume. When he is finally found dead, stabbed during his attack on the children, it is doubtful if anyone will feel any grief. In fact, Heck Tate's main reason for not taking in Boo Radley for manslaughter is that the town would treat him like a hero for killing a man they despise.

Bob Ewell has no redeeming features. He is a coward and a drunk who abuses his daughter and neglects his children, breaks the laws on poaching and spends the benefits money given to feed his family on whisky. The only way in which he can feel superior is to look down on the black community and make threats against those who reveal him for what he is.

Activity 5

Discuss your differing reactions to the presentation of the characters Boo Radley, Tom Robinson and Bob Ewell.

Other characters

Mayella Ewell

- Mayella (described as 'a thick-bodied girl accustomed to strenuous labour' *(Chapter 18)*) is the eldest of eight children and has to look after the house and the younger children while her father goes off hunting and drinks away the benefits money they receive.

- Unlike the rest of her family, she tries to keep clean and shows some appreciation of beauty by growing red geraniums in pots in the front yard.

- She is quite unused to being treated with politeness and thinks Atticus is mocking her when he calls her 'Ma'am' and 'Miss Mayella'.

- There is evidence to show that she has been beaten and possibly sexually abused by her father, but this does not excuse her from taking a man's life because she is too afraid or ashamed to tell the truth.

Atticus cross-examines Mayella in the 1962 film *To Kill a Mockingbird*

Miss Stephanie Crawford

- Maycomb's chief source of gossip, Miss Stephanie lives next door to Miss Maudie and is often the target of her sharp tongue. She goes about the neighbourhood 'doing good' *(Chapter 5)* according to Scout, but is not trusted by anyone 'with a grain of sense' *(Chapter 5)*.

- She is the chief source of rumours about Boo Radley. She also gossips about Atticus defending Tom Robinson. After the trial, she implies that Atticus planted the children in the coloured balcony to make a racial point.

- At the Missionary tea party, Miss Stephanie humiliates Scout by making fun of her court attendance in front of the other ladies.

- She is the opposite of Miss Maudie and stands for those with closed minds and prejudiced attitudes.

Heck Tate

- The first view we have of Heck Tate is when he arrives to shoot Tim Johnson, the mad dog. He is honest enough to admit it is a 'one shot job' and hand the rifle to Atticus.
- He does not share the townsfolk's view of Atticus but does come with other men to say that he is worried for Atticus's and Tom Robinson's safety.
- In court, he tries to be as truthful as he can and it is he who tells the court that Mayella's injuries were mainly on the right side of her face.
- Atticus sends for him after the children are attacked and it is Tate who finds Bob Ewell's body and the switchblade, and puts the evidence together. He says that it was not Jem who was responsible and insists that Bob Ewell fell on his knife, saying he himself had taken the switchblade from a drunk earlier on. He points out that telling the truth would have dire consequences for Boo Radley and shows Atticus that total honesty may not always be the right thing.

Mrs Henry Lafayette Dubose

- Mrs Dubose is a disagreeable old woman who sits on her porch and makes unpleasant remarks to the children as they pass. She is said to keep a Confederate pistol concealed in her wheelchair.
- When she insults Atticus and Jem takes his revenge on her camellias, he is forced to read to her every afternoon for five weeks.
- Soon after she dies, Atticus tells Jem that she had enormous courage because she had become addicted to morphine as a painkiller and was determined to be free of it before she died.
- Her role is to show the children what courage and determination can achieve and how not to react when people insult them or their father, a lesson Scout uses at the Missionary tea party.

Judge John Taylor

- Judge Taylor presides over Tom's trial.
- He cannot influence the jury, but he does appoint Atticus to defend Tom Robinson, knowing he is the only man with a chance of getting an acquittal.
- However much he may want justice done, he cannot alter the jury's determination to convict, showing that a legal system is only as good as the people in it.

Mr Link Deas

- Link Deas owns a cotton plantation and a local store. He tries to intervene on Tom Robinson's behalf during the trial and employs Helen Robinson, even though he doesn't need her, when nobody else will and defends her against Bob Ewell.
- He shows that some plantation owners were considerate towards their black employees, although to modern readers he demonstrates how powerless black people were without the support of a white man.

Mr Dolphus Raymond

- Dolphus Raymond is a wealthy local landowner who has a black mistress and a number of children of mixed race, to the scandal of Maycomb. The town can do little about him because of his wealth and he is said to be unable to change because he drinks too much whisky.
- Scout and Dill are surprised to find that his preferred drink is only Coca Cola, but he says that having a reputation as a drunk makes it easier for people to accept his lifestyle.
- His role is to show the children that morality is not always a clear line and not to accept things at face value.

Mr Walter Cunningham

- Father of the Walter Cunningham in Scout's class at school, he is a poor farmer who accepts nothing from the state, but pays in kind for Atticus's help with legal matters. He is a member of a large family of poor farmers, many of whom make up the lynch mob that faces Atticus outside the jail and is the one who calls them off. The Cunninghams are poorly educated but decent people, despite Aunt Alexandra calling them 'trash'.

Reverend Sykes

- Reverend Sykes is the main figure of authority among the black community and knows all of their good points and their failings.
- He welcomes the children on their visit. Later, he won't let his congregation out of First Purchase Church until they've collected ten dollars to help Helen Robinson.
- At the trial, it is he who looks after the children at the front of the 'coloured balcony'. It is also he who tells them to stand up when Atticus leaves the court, as a mark of respect.

Activity 6

Choose one of the minor characters from the novel and find an event or incident in the book in which they are involved. Re-tell the event or incident from their point of view as a written monologue, a diary entry or an interview for radio or a magazine.

Character map

Heck Tate: Sheriff of Maycomb; arrests Tom; saves Boo Radley from standing trial

Judge Taylor: conducts Tom's trial; appoints Atticus as defence

Bob Ewell: accuses Tom of rape; father of Mayella; unemployed drunk; threatens Atticus for defending Tom

Aunt Alexandra: sister to Atticus; aunt of Scout and Jem

Atticus Finch: lawyer defending Tom Robinson; father of Scout and Jem; brother to Alexandra and Jack; employer of Calpurnia

Tom Robinson: accused of rape; defended by Atticus; husband of Helen

Jem (Jeremy Atticus Finch): son of Atticus; brother of Scout; nephew of Alexandra and Jack

Scout (Jean Louise Finch): daughter of Atticus; sister of Jem; niece of Alexandra and Jack

Calpurnia: black housekeeper to Atticus; substitute mother to Jem and Scout

Boo (Arthur) Radley: son of Mr Nathan; brother of Nathan; protector of the children; neighbour of the Finches

Dill (Charles Baker Harris): nephew of Miss Rachel; friend of Jem; 'fiancé' of Scout

Walter Cunningham: classmate of Scout; son of Mr Walter Cunningham, a poor farmer

Nathan Radley: brother of Boo; takes over from father in keeping Boo in

Miss Rachel Haverford: aunt of Dill; neighbour of the Finches

Mr Walter Cunningham: father of Walter; member of lynch mob; poor but proud

Miss Maudie Atkinson: neighbour of the Finches; mentor to Scout and Jem

Miss Stephanie Crawford: town gossip; neighbour of Miss Maudie

Character map key

Mayella Ewell: abused daughter of Bob; accuser of Tom

Helen Robinson: Tom's wife; threatened by Bob Ewell

Reverend Sykes: pastor of First Purchase Church; collects for Helen

Mr Underwood: editor and writer of *The Maycomb Tribune*

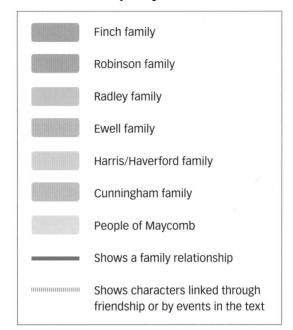

	Finch family
	Robinson family
	Radley family
	Ewell family
	Harris/Haverford family
	Cunningham family
	People of Maycomb
────	Shows a family relationship
ⅲⅲⅲⅲⅲⅲ	Shows characters linked through friendship or by events in the text

Writing about characters

Upgrade

An understanding of the characters of *To Kill a Mockingbird* is essential. Exam questions are often about a character, or sometimes a group of characters, from the novel. For example, the extract in a passage-based question may reveal something about the development of a character, whereas an essay question (not based on an extract) may ask you to trace a particular character through the novel. You need to show your knowledge and understanding of each character not just as a person, but as a created character. You therefore need to cover the following in your answer:

- what kinds of thing the author gives the character to say and how they say them
- what kinds of thing the author gives the character to do and how they do them
- what the author makes the narrator (Scout) tell us about the character
- how the author makes other characters react to them
- why the author has included the character in the novel (their role or function).

Character and viewpoint

To Kill a Mockingbird is written as a first-person narrative. The main voice in the novel is that of the adult Scout, looking back on the events of her childhood. This means that even though the child Scout is the novel's protagonist, the adult narrator uses adult language and has an adult's point of view.

The novel is written in formal language, although Scout uses many terms that are local to Alabama and the American South, and unfamiliar to British readers. However, there is also a lot of dialogue in the book and this is written in the **colloquial language** that would have been used by the children and others. Harper Lee switches from formal to colloquial language, which is often marked by the use of **elision**.

> **colloquial language** informal, everyday speech
>
> **elision** the leaving out of one or more sounds from a word to make it easier to say

---

Key quotations

If I could have explained these things to Miss Caroline, I would have saved myself some inconvenience and Miss Caroline subsequent mortification, but it was beyond my ability to explain things as well as Atticus, so I said, "You're shamin' him, Miss Caroline. Walter hasn't got a quarter at home to bring you, and you can't use any stovewood." *(Chapter 2)*

The fact that the children call their father by his first name creates another difference between them and the other children in the book, showing a different kind of relationship. Atticus himself has an educated vocabulary and speaks with what Scout refers to as 'last-will-and-testament diction' *(Chapter 3)*, causing the children to have to ask for a translation sometimes. Harper Lee shows Atticus as a lawyer in the way he argues things through logically and always sees both sides of an argument.

Harper Lee uses language as a way of defining character, giving each of her characters their own way of speaking, which helps them to stand out from one another. Miss Maudie has a very direct way of talking and is not afraid to use sarcasm, for example, at the Missionary tea party she asks, "His food doesn't stick going down, does it?" *(Chapter 24)*; Miss Rachel is recognizable by her favourite expression, "Do-o-o Jee-sus" *(Chapter 6)*; Bob Ewell's filthy talk, even in court, shows the state of his mind, while Mayella's reaction to courtesy as mocking, "I don't hafta take his sass, I aint called upon to take it" *(Chapter 18)*, reveals her background and lack of education.

Education was segregated in Alabama up until the late 1950s

Calpurnia is a good illustration of how language helps to differentiate between the separate groups in Maycomb society. Scout and Jem are surprised to hear her speaking like the other black people at First Purchase Church, when she speaks as the Finch family do while in their home. She explains it by saying that if the children spoke 'like coloured folks' at home, it would sound as odd as if she spoke like white people among her own community, who would think she was trying to be superior: "Now what if I talked white-folks' talk at church, and with my neighbours? They'd think I was puttin' on airs to beat Moses" *(Chapter 12)*.

The use of the word 'nigger', which appears frequently in the novel, is attributable to the time in which the book is set. In the 1930s, it was more acceptable than it is now, although modern readers, rightly, find it shocking. Even within the context of the time, Atticus tells Scout she is not to use it because it is 'common'. In the novel, more civilized characters refer to 'Negroes' or 'coloured folk', and Harper Lee never uses it directly. The fact that the term 'nigger lover' is hurled as abuse at Atticus says more about the people who use it in this way than it does about the even-handed Atticus. In fact, he tells Scout that such a name should not be considered an insult because it only shows the ignorance of those who use it. If using the word in your exam answers, put it in inverted commas to indicate that you are quoting from the novel.

Atmosphere and symbolism

Harper Lee uses description to create a vivid picture of people and events in the novel, using a number of colourful **metaphors** and **similes**. For example, when Scout tells us, 'Talking to Francis gave me the sensation of settling slowly to the bottom of the ocean' *(Chapter 9)*, we know exactly the dull, leaden boredom she is feeling or when Scout describes how Miss Maudie 'spread her fingers on her knees and settled her bridgework' *(Chapter 22)*, we can see her doing it. There are many similar phrases throughout the book, such as this one referring to Miss Caroline: 'She looked and smelled like a peppermint drop' *(Chapter 2)*.

Harper Lee also uses her descriptive powers to build up tension at moments in the book, such as when the children venture into the Radley back garden and when they are followed by Bob Ewell at the end of the book. At these times she makes use of the senses to create a suspenseful **atmosphere** and to place us in the scene with the characters; for example in Chapter 28, Scout says, 'what I thought were trees rustling was the soft swish of cotton on cotton' and 'I felt the sand go cold under my feet'.

The author cleverly uses **symbolism** in the novel, with the mockingbird as a symbol of innocence and Atticus's shooting of the rabid dog as a metaphor for his attempt to dispel the madness of racism. She also uses phrases such as "climb into his skin and walk around in it" *(Chapter 3)* as a metaphor for seeing things from another person's point of view, while Mayella Ewell's geraniums represent a frustrated desire for order and beauty in her life.

The mockingbird has captured the imagination as a symbol of innocence and is the state bird of five southern states in the USA

Activity 1

a) Work in pairs on a copy of the scene where the children trespass in the Radley's garden (Chapter 6). Using different colours, highlight the following:

- all the words and phrases to do with **sight**, **touch** or **hearing** that help to build tension

- all the verbs that show ways of **moving**.

b) Now write three paragraphs on how Harper Lee uses language to create tension in this episode.

When describing Boo Radley as Maycomb sees him, Harper Lee makes use of gothic ideas that are familiar from horror stories and films. Boo is mentioned first as a 'malevolent phantom' *(Chapter 1)*, while the Radley place is described in the same way as a haunted house or one in which frightening things happen – as indeed they do, but in a different way.

Humour is another feature of Harper Lee's writing. She uses it mainly through Scout and sometimes through Miss Maudie or Atticus.

atmosphere the mood created by a piece of writing

metaphor a comparison of one thing to another to make a description more vivid; a metaphor states that one thing *is* the other

simile a comparison of one thing to another to make a description more vivid, using the words 'like' or 'as' to make the comparison

symbolism using something to represent a concept, idea or theme in a novel

Writing about language

Upgrade

An understanding of the language choices that Harper Lee has made in *To Kill a Mockingbird* is necessary, as together with structure and form, they contribute to the writer's presentation of ideas, characters, themes and setting.

Courage

The novel explores different kinds of courage. As they grow up, the children learn about personal courage, as well as witnessing the courage of adults in various situations.

The courage of children

Both Jem and Scout have a sense of honour and pride which makes them brave, although in childish ways. They face things they are scared of and often pretend not to be scared in order to save face.

> **Key quotations**
>
> Our first raid came to pass only because Dill bet Jem *The Grey Ghost* against two Tom Swifts that Jem wouldn't get any farther than the Radley gate. In all his life, Jem had never declined a dare. *(Chapter 1)*

Jem shows courage in his acceptance of Dill's dare to touch the Radley house. He is afraid, as shown by his mad dash and by his screaming at Scout when she is spilled out of the tyre at the bottom of the steps, but he still makes a foray to rescue the tyre. The children also show courage of a sort when they steal into the Radley garden at night, but Jem shows it more when he returns for his trousers alone.

Scout shows courage by fighting anybody who upsets her, but most of all when she is defending Atticus. She jumps on Francis when he says horrible things about her father on Christmas Day. However, she shows even more courage by not fighting with Cecil Jacobs because Atticus has asked her not to.

Physical courage

The children admire Atticus when they see him shoot Tim Johnson with a single shot and learn that he was known as 'One-Shot Finch' *(Chapter 10)*. The image of Atticus as a lonely figure in the street, with a rabid dog coming towards him, is one that stays with Scout and comes back to her when she remembers him folding his newspaper and pushing back his hat outside the Maycomb jail. His confrontation with the lynch mob is another demonstration of physical courage. Scout is surprised to see fear in his eyes, although it is fear for his children not himself; it is her innocent lack of fear, because she doesn't understand the situation, that saves them all.

Moral courage

Moral courage, which often involves some physical courage, is when a person does what they know to be the right thing, regardless of the consequences. Atticus tries to teach the children what true courage means through the incident with Mrs Dubose. She is unpleasant and physically repulsive but she frees herself from her morphine addiction, with the children's help, before she dies.

"I wanted you to see what real courage is, instead of getting the idea that courage is a man with a gun in his hand. It's when you know you're licked before you begin but you begin anyway and you see it through no matter what. You rarely win, but sometimes you do." *(Chapter 11)*

One of the 'Little Rock Nine' braves a hostile crowd of students to attend classes at Little Rock Central High School, Arkansas in 1957

Although he is applying these words to Mrs Dubose, they also describe what Atticus himself does in defending Tom Robinson. He knows there is no chance of winning a case that depends on a black man's word against that of a white man and woman, but he does his very best at some cost to himself and his family.

Social courage

Scout learns about a different kind of courage from Aunt Alexandra and Miss Maudie. In the middle of the Missionary tea party, they learn that Tom Robinson has been shot dead while trying to escape from prison. Aunt Alexandra is very upset because she can see how much Tom's death has affected Atticus. Scout imagines the scene at the prison and starts to shake uncontrollably. She is ordered to stop by Miss Maudie, who tells Aunt Alexandra they must carry on. The three of them manage to return to the tea party and continue being good hostesses in spite of their feelings.

Aunt Alexandra looked across the room at me and smiled. She looked at a tray of cookies on the table and nodded at them. I carefully picked up the tray and watched myself walk to Mrs Merriweather. With my very best company manners, I asked her if she would have some.

After all, if Aunty could be a lady at a time like this, so could I. *(Chapter 24)*

Activity 1

With a partner, discuss when the characters below show courage.

- Boo Radley
- Link Deas
- Mr Underwood
- Heck Tate

Decide what kind of courage they show and find evidence to support your ideas. Make notes that you can use for revision.

Good and evil

The novel also explores contrasting ideas of good and evil. The main evil is the racial prejudice that permeates the town and the whole state of Alabama. It is a systematized form of evil, which has become so much part of the residents' way of life that many people see it as normal. Atticus tells Uncle Jack:

> **Key quotations**
>
> "You know what's going to happen as well as I do, Jack, and I hope and pray I can get Jem and Scout through it without bitterness, and most of all, without catching Maycomb's usual disease. Why reasonable people go stark raving mad when anything involving a Negro comes up, is something I don't pretend to understand... I just hope that Jem and Scout come to me for their answers instead of listening to the town." *(Chapter 9)*

This racial prejudice is countered by the small handful of people, particularly Atticus, who fight against it.

Activity 2

Read the following quotation.

> **Key quotations**
>
> "The witnesses for the state, with the exception of the sheriff of Maycomb County, have presented themselves to you gentlemen, to this court, in the cynical confidence that their testimony would not be doubted, confident that you gentlemen would go along with them on the assumption – the evil assumption – that *all* Negroes lie, that *all* Negroes are basically immoral beings, that *all* Negro men are not to be trusted around our women, an assumption one associates with minds of their calibre." *(Chapter 18)*

a) With a partner, make a list of the ways this 'evil assumption' is shown in the novel.

b) Make a list of the people who try to fight racial prejudice and the ways in which they do it.

c) Present your findings on a large sheet of paper for display. You could use pictures of the characters and suitable quotations, as well as your own comments.

Much of the evil in the novel stems from Bob Ewell, a man who abuses his daughter and encourages her to have an innocent man sentenced to death. The conviction of Tom Robinson is not enough for him, however, because he then goes after anyone he feels was against him. He spits in Atticus's face and threatens him, he breaks into Judge Taylor's house and he stalks Helen Robinson. Even so, Atticus tries to see things from his point of view:

Key quotations

"Jem, see if you can stand in Bob Ewell's shoes a minute. I destroyed his last shred of credibility at that trial, if he had any to begin with. The man had to have some kind of comeback, his kind always does. So if spitting in my face and threatening me saved Mayella Ewell one extra beating, that's something I'll gladly take. He had to take it out on somebody and I'd rather it be me than that houseful of children out there." *(Chapter 23)*

Atticus's tolerance and goodness blind him to the depth of evil that Bob Ewell harbours and the fact that his own children might become a target for murder. In the end they are saved, not by their father's foresight, but by the town's other target for evil behaviour – Boo Radley.

At the beginning of the novel, the children are innocent. They feel safe in Maycomb and trust the people around them. Their fears are of Boo Radley and Mrs Dubose – neither of whom justify their feelings. As the story progresses, the children gradually learn about evil and cruelty through experience.

Their first experience comes through the Radleys' and the town's treatment of Boo. As children, they see him as a 'malevolent phantom' *(Chapter 1)*, who might 'get them' in some unspecified way and they are both frightened and fascinated in equal measure. They do not stop to consider that their games and their attempts to get Boo to come out could be unkind, despite Atticus's clear instructions.

In fact, Boo Radley was confined to the house by his father, hidden from view, and forbidden communication with the outside world. Even Boo's attempts to befriend the children by leaving gifts in the oak tree are stopped by his brother. When Scout finally meets Boo and realizes what he is like, she feels sad that they never repaid him for his kindness.

Activity 3

With a partner, look at the section in Chapter 31 from 'Daylight... in my mind, the night faded... ' to 'Just standing on the Radley porch was enough'.

a) Discuss what this extract tells us about Scout's new understanding of Boo Radley.

b) How far does it give the reader a new perspective on the way Boo was treated by his family and by the townsfolk?

c) Why do you think Harper Lee included this episode in her novel?

The Mockingbird

Boo and Tom are destroyed as the story unfolds. Tom Robinson is accused of a crime that he did not commit because Mayella Ewell needed to get rid of the evidence of her sexual desire for someone forbidden to her by social rules. Mr Underwood compares his killing to 'the senseless slaughter of songbirds' (Chapter 25). Boo Radley is punished beyond reason by his father after indulging in teenage high spirits, while his peers were sent to a school where they prospered. Both Tom and Boo represent the harmless mockingbirds of the novel's title, which sing for pleasure.

Jem finds that faith in humanity is hard to sustain when innocents like Tom and Boo are destroyed. However, by the end of the novel, Scout understands the significance of the association when she tells Atticus that Boo Radley should not be arrested for the murder of Bob Ewell because 'it'd be sort of like shootin' a mockingbird' (Chapter 30).

Family

The importance of family life is demonstrated mainly through the Finch family, but other families are portrayed as well, with differing sets of values.

The Cunninghams are poverty stricken but refuse to take charity and insist on paying with goods for whatever they use. They are also scrupulously clean and their old clothes are patched and mended. They are a contrast to the Ewells, who live like animals and are filthy and uncouth. Bob Ewell drinks the benefit money they receive, poaches out of season and abuses his daughter, who is the only one to make an effort by planting and taking care of her geraniums.

Thousands of American families had to scrape through the Great Depression in the 1930s on virtually nothing, but still managed to care for their children

The Radleys are unsociable and rarely go out. Mr Radley imprisoned Arthur (Boo) in the house for a minor offence and his son Nathan continues the cruelty after his death, even cementing the tree hole where Boo leaves little gifts for the children. Dill's parents show a different kind of cruelty, taking no interest in him and finding him a nuisance, although they give him material things.

In contrast, Atticus cares for his children, taking a real interest in them and spending time talking to and reading with them. He is in tune with their moods and they respect him and value his good opinion. He also supports Calpurnia in her role as substitute mother to them.

Religion and the notion of sin

Although this is not a major theme in the novel, religion underpins many of the attitudes held by the people of Maycomb. Throughout the story, Atticus's behaviour is an example of true Christian values. The Finch family are Methodists and attend church every Sunday, although Atticus has no objection to the children going to First Purchase with Calpurnia.

Miss Maudie is a Baptist, as are many of the other inhabitants of Maycomb, but she is a tolerant woman who keeps her distance from the 'foot-washing Baptists', who tell her she will burn in hell because she spends time making her garden beautiful. She tells Scout that these people believe that anything that gives pleasure is a sin.

Atticus tells the children, *"... it's a sin to kill a mockingbird" (Chapter 10)* and Miss Maudie explains that this is because mockingbirds do nothing but sing for people. Atticus's idea of sin is very different from that of Mrs Merriweather, who says the Mrunas live in *"sin and squalor" (Chapter 24)*, although in fact they have a communal life that many people would consider ideal.

In Chapter 25, Mr Underwood applies the term 'sin' more fittingly in his editorial for the *Maycomb Tribune* after Tom's death where he *'simply figured it was a sin to kill cripples, be they standing, sitting, or escaping'* and compares it to *'the senseless slaughter of songbirds'*. At the end of the novel, Heck Tate insists to Atticus, *"To my way of thinkin', Mr Finch, taking the one man who's done you and this town a great service an' draggin' him with his shy ways into the limelight – to me, that's a sin. It's a sin and I'm not about to have it on my head."*

Although they claim to be Christians, many of the town's inhabitants are not very Christian in their treatment of others. Their attitude towards black people, Boo Radley and Dolphus Raymond is intolerant and prejudiced. In the novel, religion is often associated with hypocrisy and a narrow-minded outlook. First Purchase seems to be the exception when the Reverend Sykes makes a collection for Helen Robinson, although Scout notes the same negative attitude towards females as in her own church.

Education

Scout looks forward to school but even on her first day she is disillusioned by the educational standards she encounters. Her class includes many children who are repeating the first grade because they miss classes when they are needed to work on the farms. Miss Caroline Fisher, the teacher, tells Scout that she must learn to read by the Dewey system and that Atticus must not read with her any more, even though she is a fluent reader already. She is also told that she must not write, as she is not supposed to learn that skill until the second grade. Consequently, she becomes determined not to go back to school.

Miss Fisher is fresh from college and inexperienced. She is also a stranger to the area so doesn't know or understand the local ways – and is therefore suspicious. She is not interested in treating the children as individuals or in teaching methods that will suit their experiences of life and seems insensitive to their needs: **"Now you tell your father not to teach you any more. It's best to begin reading with a fresh mind. You tell him I'll take over from here and try to undo the damage –"** *(Chapter 2)*.

Scout finds second grade every bit as boring as first grade. The state education system lets the children down badly, but at least they are better off than the black children, who don't seem to have a school at all.

The teachers share the prejudiced attitudes and hypocrisy of the rest of the town as shown in the Current Affairs lesson, when Miss Gates becomes quite heated about Hitler's persecution of the Jews, but makes racist remarks outside the courtroom at Tom Robinson's trial.

The children learn far more about people, values and life from Atticus, Miss Maudie and Calpurnia than they ever do at school. Both Atticus and Calpurnia have strong moral principles and enforce them. Some of the children's most important lessons come from their experiences of life in Maycomb and the behaviour of its population. The people they respect, such as Miss Maudie, are good role models and, even though she has a difficult relationship with Aunt Alexandra, Scout learns more from her than she could have imagined.

Activity 4

Working in a small group, each person should choose a different theme from the novel.

a) Make a spider diagram or a concept map to show how your theme is explored though the characters and events.

b) Then make a timeline to show how your theme develops through the novel, giving it more or less space according to its importance at different times.

c) Finally, display all your group's diagrams or maps on a large sheet of paper, using appropriate headings and quotations.

Writing about themes

Upgrade

The way you approach themes in the exam will depend on the question you have been asked. The question(s) may well be on a particular theme, such as education, the family or racial prejudice. In this case you need to show how the author brings out these themes through the different characters and events.

Even if the question is not specifically about themes in the novel, you should still show that you have understood them. For example, if you are writing about the character of Miss Maudie, you can show how Harper Lee tackles the themes of courage, religion and prejudice through the way Miss Maudie behaves, what she says and what Scout tells us about her.

You should also look at how a theme develops as the novel progresses. For example, does racial prejudice become more important by the middle of the book than at the beginning? Is it more or less important by the end of the novel? Do certain events in the story make the theme more dominant? For example, how does the trial bring the theme of racial prejudice to the foreground? How is it viewed by different characters at different times in the novel?

Exam skills

Understanding the question

Look at the number of marks awarded for each section of the question. Then divide the time you have available to write the answer in proportion to the marks. For example, if you have 45 minutes to answer a two-part question where part a) is worth 7 marks and part b) is worth 20 marks, it is clear that you should spend no more than ten minutes on part a) and 30 minutes on part b), allowing five minutes for planning. If the two parts are worth ten marks each, you should aim to spend twenty minutes on each part.

Try to approach the question in a methodical way. Start by identifying what the question is actually asking you to do: you could underline the key words and phrases, and note down what they mean. Examiners use certain words and phrases quite often. Learn what they each mean and you will know what you need to write about.

'Explore' means look at all the different aspects of something. For example, 'Explore how the author makes Tom Robinson a sympathetic character' means you need to look at his character as shown at his church, as seen by his employer, as shown to the reader during the trial; then you need to look at how he is treated by the Ewells, by the lynch mob and by Mr Gilmer and the jury in court, what happens to him in prison and the reactions of different people to that.

'How does the author... ' or **'show how... '** means explain the techniques the author uses to create an effect. For example, 'How does Lee make this episode tense?' means you need to look at how she builds up suspense or tension in the way she structures the scene; how she uses language to make the reader feel excitement or fear; and how she uses the reactions of various characters in the scene to make the reader see, hear and feel what the characters experience.

'Present' and **'portray'** are similar words for looking at a character and they mean not only what the character is like, but also what devices the author uses to show us what they are like. For example, 'How is Miss Maudie Atkinson presented/portrayed?' means you need to say how she is described; what the author makes her say and do, and why; how the author shows other people reacting to her; and how Lee shows her as important to the story.

'In what ways... ' means look at different sides of something. For example, 'In what ways are Bob and Mayella Ewell significant?' means you need to look at more than just their role as accusors of Tom Robinson, although this is undoubtedly their major role. You need to explain their social function as 'white trash' despised by Maycomb; the contrast between them and the Cunninghams; their dysfunctional family life due to Bob's work–shy nature and drinking habits; Mayella's loneliness and aspirations to something better; the fact that their prejudice comes from ignorance and poverty (whereas the ladies of the tea party have no such excuse).

'What role... ' means write about not just the character and how they are shown but also about their function in the novel. For example, 'What role does Boo Radley play?' means you have to write about his character and how it is shown, but also why he is in the novel at all (you could imagine the novel without him). He is a 'malevolent phantom', 'a ghost' and a mysterious gothic figure but also a shy recluse who has been made a non-person, a friend and ultimately saviour to the children; he is a mockingbird figure who shows that prejudice is directed towards anyone 'different' (like Mr Dolphus Raymond) not just those of a different colour. He is also used to bring out the hypocrisy of rigid religious views in his family.

'Explain' or **'comment on'** invite you to give your response to something in as much detail as you can. For example, 'Explain the importance of racism in one part of the novel' means you should write about the way Maycomb society behaves towards black people in general, and Tom Robinson in particular, either before or after the trial, relating it to the context of southern America in the 1930s, lynch mobs and the Ku Klux Klan. What the children observe is important here, as are Atticus's reactions, and you should give your ideas about why Harper Lee makes this such a big issue in the story.

Look at the question below. The key words and phrases have been highlighted and explained.

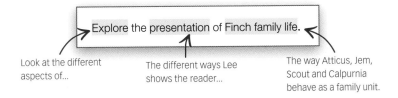

Explore the presentation of Finch family life.

Look at the different aspects of...

The different ways Lee shows the reader...

The way Atticus, Jem, Scout and Calpurnia behave as a family unit.

You are being asked to do a number of things in this question. You need to look at:

- how Harper Lee brings out the relationship between Atticus and the children
- how she shows the relationship between Calpurnia and the children
- how she shows the relationship between Jem and Scout and the other children
- how she makes the reader see the family against the background of prejudice and gossip in the town of Maycomb.

> ## Activity 1
>
> With a partner, look at the question below.
>
> **Show how Boo Radley is important to the novel as a whole.**
>
> **a)** Highlight or underline the key words and phrases and then describe what you are being asked to do.
>
> **b)** Make a bullet list of things you need to do to answer the question.

Planning your answer

It is worth taking five minutes to plan your answer before you start to write it. Plan an effective structure for your answer and add pointers for the information you need to include in it. Then when you write the actual answer, you will be free to concentrate on your writing style and to make sure you have used the correct terminology and included evidence to support your points.

Examiners always make the point that candidates who use their own ideas about the text produce fresher and more interesting answers than candidates who have prepared possible answers to almost every question in advance. So, the key is to practise planning answers to a variety of questions, not to actually write the answers during your revision.

Below are several different ways of planning an essay. Any of these plans would help you to gather ideas for your answer and clearly set out the information you need to include.

Lists

You can list points that you want to include, perhaps with a brief note of the evidence you will use. This is what the list might look like for the following question:

> Explore the presentation of Finch family life.

- ✔ Intro – who is in the Finch family and what relation they are
- ✔ Atticus as a parent – how his legal training influences how he deals with the children (always sees both sides; always answers questions truthfully)
- ✔ What he teaches them (tolerance, respect, compassion, nature of courage, understanding of others, etc.)
- ✔ How he teaches them (through example as well as what he says)
- ✔ Atticus as the moral conscience of Maycomb (prepared to face physical danger and unpopularity for what he believes in, and even risk his children)

✔ The way the family stick together (against the lynch mob and insults from others, at the trial, after Tom Robinson's death)

✔ How they represent hope for a better future (showing a different attitude towards black people, making a stand for equality under the law – one juror at least tried to acquit)

Spider diagrams

You could also put your points into a spider diagram like this, adding more boxes if you wish:

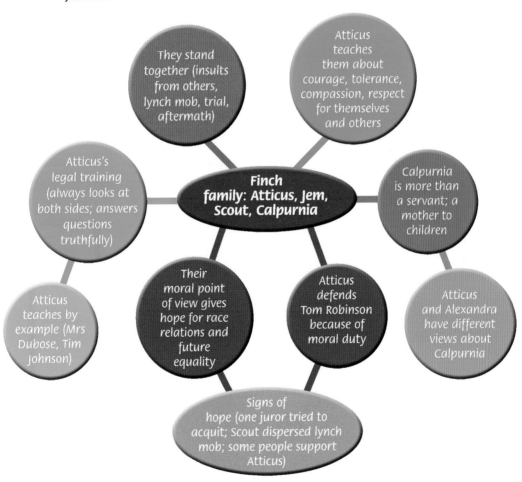

Concept maps

You could make your points in a concept map like this, adding more boxes if you wish:

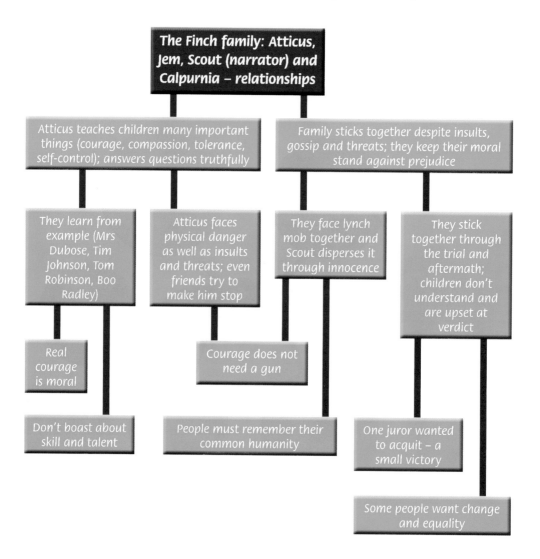

Writing your answer

When you have a good plan, you will know what you need to write and have thought about how to structure your ideas. For the example question, start with a brief introduction to the Finch family and their relationships and finish with the idea that they represent a spark of hope for the future of equality in Maycomb.

You also need to pay close attention to the quality of your written communication in your answer, including your spelling, punctuation and grammar. Your answer should show your knowledge and understanding of:

- what the author is saying
- how the author is saying it
- how the setting and context influence the author and reader (where relevant).

Using Point, Evidence, Explanation (PEE)

Examiners want to see that you can support your ideas in a thoughtful way and that you have based them on what the author says and means. For example, you might make the point:

Atticus teaches his children by example rather than just telling them what to do.

Your evidence for this might be:

When he shoots Tim Johnson, the children find out that he has a reputation as 'One-Shot Finch' although he has never mentioned it.

Your explanation might be:

This shows that Atticus doesn't want them to think that shooting things is a skill to be proud of and this fits in with his idea that courage is not "a man with a gun in his hands".

Using quotations

This is an important part of using evidence in your answer. Examiners want to see that you can select appropriate quotations that back up the point you are making. When you make a point, ask yourself: 'How do I know this?' Usually it will be because of something the author has written – this is the quotation you need.

For example, you might make the point:

> Scout is intelligent and she absorbs most of what Atticus tells her.

How do you know this? Well, there might be a number of quotations you could choose, but here is one:

> At the end of the book, when Atticus asks if she understands why Heck Tate will not prosecute Boo Radley, she tells him "it'd be sort of like shootin' a mockingbird".

By choosing this quotation you will show that you:

- can select a relevant quotation to support your answer
- have understood how Scout is intelligent and how she has listened to Atticus
- have understood that this relates to an important theme of the book.

Examiners will reward you for using well-chosen quotations in your answer, but if you want to show skills of a higher level, try to use embedded quotations. These are quotations that are part of your main text, marked only by speech marks. If you look at the examples above, you will see how this is done.

What not to do in an exam answer

✗ Do not begin with introductions such as 'In this answer I am going to show...'. Instead just start straight in and do the showing as you go. Make sure your introduction addresses the question and that you go back to it in your conclusion.

✗ Do not write lengthy paragraphs about the background to the novel. You may think the history of slavery is important to racial prejudice in the novel, but show this briefly while you focus on answering the actual question.

✗ Do not focus on some parts of the set extract and ignore others. Always answer on the passage as a whole.

✗ Do not write a long introduction showing what you know about the author. Make just a brief reference and only if it is relevant to a point you are making.

✗ If you are responding to a set extract, do not refer extensively to other parts of the novel, unless you are asked to do so.

✗ Do not go into the exam with a prepared list of points and write about them if they are not relevant to the question.

✗ Do not mention literary techniques the author has used in the set extract just for the sake of it. Only do so if you can show what effect it creates.

✗ Do not run out of time to finish your answer – a plan will help you avoid this. It is better to focus on a detailed answer on a small part of the text than to try and make lots of different points and make none thoroughly.

✗ Do not try to write everything you know about the text – make sure that you only choose things that are relevant to the question.

Achieving the best marks

Upgrade

To achieve high marks, you will need to do the following:

• show an assured or perceptive understanding of the book's themes/ideas

• show a pertinent or convincing response to the text

• select evidence that is relevant, detailed and sustained

• make references to context that are pertinent, convincing and supported by sustained, relevant textual reference

• use sentences that are sophisticated and varied; show precise control of expression and meaning; use a full range of punctuation and spelling that is consistently accurate.

In practice this means that you need to read more than just the set text. Ideally you should read some critical guides to the text and add their interpretation to your own response and ideas about the book.

You need to show that you have understood the book on more than one level. On the surface, it is a story about the unfair trial of a black man in a small town in Alabama in the 1930s, told from the viewpoint of someone who was a child at the time, Scout. If you look more deeply, it is a passionate argument for equality and humanity, as represented by Atticus Finch.

You will have to show that you understand the way in which the narrative works and why Harper Lee chose to use an adult narrator telling the story from a child's point of view. Although Lee claims that Maycomb is not her home town of Monroeville, it bears remarkable similarities, as she does to Scout, Atticus does to her father and Dill does to her friend, Truman Capote. How might this affect the way in which she depicts the setting and characters?

You will also need to show not just that you have understood the symbolism that Lee uses, but how, in your view, she applies it and why she uses it.

In addition you will need to use appropriate literary terminology correctly to make your answers more precise and show that you have a sophisticated writing style.

Sample questions

1

Foundation Tier

Harper Lee: *To Kill a Mockingbird*

Read the passage and then answer the questions that follow.

Look at the extract towards the end of Chapter 6 from 'Dill stopped and let Jem go ahead... ' to '... were at the back steps before Jem would let us pause to rest.'

a) What does this extract show about the children's attitude to the Radley place and those who live there?

b) What is the importance of Boo Radley in the book as a whole?

You should think about:

* the attitude of people in Maycomb towards Boo Radley

* Boo's relationship with the children.

2

Higher Tier

Harper Lee: *To Kill a Mockingbird*

Read the passage and then answer the questions which follow.

Look at the extract at the beginning of Chapter 9 from "You can just take that back, boy!" to "... I couldn't even tell you or Jem not to do something again."

a) What does this extract show about the relationship between Scout and Atticus?

b) How important is Atticus's defence of Tom Robinson in the book as a whole?

3

Foundation Tier

Lee: *To Kill a Mockingbird*

Answer either (a) or (b).

(a) What part does Miss Maudie play in the children's education? How important do you think she is to the Finch family? Give reasons for your opinions.

In your answer you should consider the presentation of:

• what she tells the children about Atticus and others in Maycomb

• how she behaves towards them

• the way she reacts to events surrounding the trial of Tom Robinson.

(b) *Look at the extract in the middle of Chapter 17 from 'Every town the size of Maycomb had families like the Ewells' to 'People said they were Mayella Ewell's.'*

With reference to the extract and elsewhere in the novel, show how the children's views of the Ewell family **change**.

In your answer you should consider the presentation of:

• Atticus's views of the Ewells

• how they are shown during the trial

• Bob Ewell's behaviour after the trial.

4

Higher Tier

Lee: *To Kill a Mockingbird*

Answer either (a) or (b).

(a) With reference to the ways Lee presents Miss Maudie, show how far you would agree that she is important to the Finch family.

(b) *Look at the section in Chapter 17 from 'Every town the size of Maycomb had families like the Ewells' to 'People said they were Mayella Ewell's.'*

With reference to the ways Lee presents the Ewells in the printed extract and elsewhere in the novel, show how far you would agree that the children's views of them **change**.

5

Foundation Tier

To Kill a Mockingbird

Either a)

Tom Robinson could be considered as a 'mockingbird' in the novel. Explain how he might fit this role. You should consider:

- the way he behaves towards Mayella Ewell

- the evidence he gives in court

- the attitude of the white people towards him

- what happens to him later in the story.

You may include other ideas of your own.

Use **evidence** to support your answer.

Or b)

What part does Dill play in the novel as a whole? You should consider:

- the stories he makes up

- his fascination with Boo Radley

- why he runs away from home

- the way he behaves at the trial.

You may include other ideas of your own.

Use **evidence** to support your answer.

6

Higher Tier

To Kill a Mockingbird

Either a)

Explore the importance of families in the novel.

You **must** consider the context of the novel.

Use **evidence** to support your answer.

Or b)

How is the character of Miss Maudie presented in the novel?

You **must** consider the context of the novel.

Use **evidence** to support your answer.

7

Foundation Tier

HARPER LEE: *To Kill a Mockingbird*

Either a)

Look at the extract towards the end of Chapter 15 from 'There was a smell of stale whiskey and pig-pen about... ' to "You got fifteen seconds to get 'em outa here."

How does Harper Lee make this episode so tense and exciting in the novel?

You should consider:

- the way the writer describes what the children see and hear
- how Atticus and Jem behave
- what Scout says and does.

Or b)

What are your feelings about Tom Robinson and the way he is treated in the novel?

Remember to support your ideas with details from the novel.

8

Higher Tier

HARPER LEE: *To Kill a Mockingbird*

Either a)

Look at the extract in Chapter 15 from 'There was a smell of stale whisky and pig-pen about... ' to "You got fifteen seconds to get 'em outa here."

How does Harper Lee make this such a tense and exciting scene in the novel?

Or b)

Explore how Harper Lee makes Tom Robinson such a sympathetic figure in the novel.

Remember to support your ideas with details from the novel.

9

Foundation Tier

To Kill a Mockingbird

Answer both parts of (a) and **either** part (b) **or** part (c).

(a) *Look at the extract at the end of Chapter 26 from 'Jem was worn out from a day's water-carrying... ' to the end.*

   (i) What do you think about the way Jem speaks and behaves here?

   (ii) What do you think about the way Scout speaks and behaves here?

Either

(b) What do you think about Atticus Finch?

Think about:

- what you learn about him as a person
- his relationship with the children
- how he defends Tom Robinson
- anything else you think important.

Or

(c) Atticus tells the children that "it's a sin to kill a mockingbird". Write about two or three times in the novel when the children see how this applies to people.

10

Higher Tier

To Kill a Mockingbird

Answer question (a) and **either** part (b) **or** part (c).

(a) *Look at the extract at the end of Chapter 26 from 'Jem was worn out from a day's water-carrying... ' to the end.*

With close reference to the extract, show how Harper Lee brings out the relationship between Jem and Scout.

Either

(b) Show how the character of Atticus Finch is important to the novel as a whole.

Or

(c) Atticus tells the children "it's a sin to kill a mockingbird". Show how they learn that this applies to people as well, at different points in the novel.

Sample answers

Sample answer 1

Below is a sample response from a **Foundation Tier** student, together with examiner comments, to the following general question on the novel:

> What part does Tom Robinson play in the novel as a whole?

Starts with Tom, but only as 'the accused' rather than his role generally.

This comment is made too early and would be better later on.

Quotation is relevant but not in context.

It would have been better to start the answer here.

Point could have been expanded to show Tom's reputation at church and as a family man.

Shows knowledge of the context and danger Tom is in, but not well integrated.

This is the right place for the point but it is now repetition.

This is more about Atticus than Tom; could have mentioned Tom's lack of power.

This is just an account of Tom's evidence with little comment, e.g. on why this was such a bad situation for him – and for Mayella.

The quotation is in context, but not explained.

Tom Robinson is a black man who has been unfairly accused of raping Mayella Ewell. Harper Lee does not tell us much about him until the trial scene when we see that he has a useless left arm, which means he could not be guilty as Mayella was beaten up by a left-handed person. I know this because Scout says 'Atticus was trying to show, it seemed to me, that Mr Ewell could have beaten up Mayella.'

All we know about Tom Robinson up to the trial is that he goes to First Purchase Church and has a wife called Helen and some children. Atticus goes to sit outside Maycomb Jail to protect Tom on the night before the trial and it is a good job he does because a crowd of men arrive outside. This is a lynch mob, who were people that went around hanging black people from trees instead of waiting for a court to give them a trial. This is what they want to do to Tom, but Atticus is in the way. The children arrive and run up to Atticus in front of the men. In the end, Scout talks to Mr Cunningham about his son and they all go away.

In the court, when Mayella points to Tom as the one who raped her, he stands up and everyone sees his left arm is useless. This means it could not have been him who beat up Mayella. When Atticus pushes her to tell the truth, she bursts into tears and refuses to answer any more questions. When Atticus asks Tom what happened, he says Mayella asked him to come inside and get a box off the top of a wardrobe and then she grabbed him and kissed him. Then Mr Ewell looked through the window and Tom was afraid, so he ran away. He says, "Mr Finch, if you were a nigger like me, you'd be scared, too!"

When Mr Gilmer asked Tom why he helped Mayella, he says he felt sorry for her which was not a good answer as people thought it was wrong for a black man to feel sorry for a white person. The way Mr Gilmer treats Tom is horrible and it makes Dill cry, so he and Scout have to go out. When they go back in, Atticus is making his speech to the jury. He tries to show that it was obvious the Ewells were lying and they thought people would be on their side because of the way they think of black people. He says they think the jury will assume Tom did it because "all Negroes lie, that all Negroes are basically immoral beings, that all Negro men are not to be trusted round our women."

The Ewells are right because the jury do convict Tom even though it is clear he is innocent. Atticus tells Tom they will appeal and they stand a good chance, but Tom does not wait for the appeal and he is shot seventeen times while trying to escape. Tom is like the mockingbird in the book's title because he only tried to help Mayella and he ended up dead for no reason.

This is a good point with some attempt to explain it.

There is no explanation about how Mr Gilmer is horrible or why Dill cries.

Good point about Atticus's summing up and the Ewells' cynical view.

Well-chosen and well-embedded quotation, which just needed some explanation.

Good point about the mockingbird symbol with some explanation.

The candidate shows understanding of the story and Tom's position, but the essay is not well structured and the points are not always relevant. It doesn't really answer the question and there is insufficient textual evidence or explanation.

Sample answer 2

The sample answer below is from a **Higher Tier** student to the same general question:

> What part does Tom Robinson play in the novel as a whole?

Opening sentence directly addresses the question.

Relates question to theme of family and to central characters.

Well-chosen quotation to support point, properly embedded.

Tom Robinson is the character designed to bring out the true depth of racial prejudice in Maycomb. His trial and the events surrounding it are a difficult test for Atticus and his children. Atticus tries to make Scout understand why he is defending Tom, "I'm simply defending a Negro – his name's Tom Robinson. He lives in that little settlement beyond the town dump. He's a member of Calpurnia's church, and Cal knows his family well. She says they're clean-living folks." This also tells us that Tom is a decent man, which is necessary if he is to gain sympathy.

Shows Lee building up an impression of Tom.

This suggestion is reinforced at First Purchase Church when Reverend Sykes announces that Tom "has been a faithful member of First Purchase since he was a boy". This suggests that Tom is a good Christian and that he has principles and morals, especially since the minister has no hesitation in denouncing any 'sinners' among his congregation. This adds to the reader's impression of, and sympathy for, Tom. Rev. Sykes is making a collection for Helen, Tom's wife, and his children, which makes the reader realize the hardship being caused to an innocent family. This is also when we discover the allegation against Tom when Calpurnia tells Scout, "Old Mr Bob Ewell accused him of rapin' his girl an' had him arrested an' put in jail–" For a black man to rape a white woman was a capital offence and the reader then knows what Tom is facing, which raises the stakes.

The point is well made and perceptive about the author's intentions.

Well-selected second point linked to first by way of quotation.

Shows wider reading; other opinions and criticisms being put forward.

Harper Lee has been accused of making the black characters in the book, and Tom Robinson in particular, too passive and dependent on the white people around them. It must be remembered that she wrote the book at the beginning of the 1960s when the Civil Rights movement was in its infancy and that she was writing as a white member of a southern community. The novel is set in the 1930s at a time when black people faced discrimination in every area, so this passive attitude is probably realistic, as they were dependent on whites for jobs and money.

Individual and thoughtful response to criticisms based on contextual knowledge.

Return to addressing the question directly keeps answer focused.

Tom's role is that of victim, first of a lynch mob, who come for him the night before the trial. Their intention of hanging Tom is frustrated by Atticus and the children, but this incident demonstrates the kind of justice that a black man accused of raping a white woman could expect. He is then a victim of the biased legal system, which was weighted against black people. The jury consists of the same kind of farmers who made up the lynch mob. They are all white because only voters could be jurors and black people did not have a vote.

Succinct, appropriate and integrated use of context.

Tom's trial is the central focus of the novel and it was based, to some extent, on the Scotsboro' trials which also concerned the alleged rape of white women by black men. In spite of Atticus's brilliant defence, which clearly demonstrates that the Ewells are lying, Tom is convicted, as Atticus knew he would be. In his summing up, Atticus tells the jury that the Ewells knew the jurors would be on their side because they would accept "the assumption – the evil assumption – that all Negroes lie, that all Negroes are basically immoral beings, that all Negro men are not to be trusted around our women." He argues for the principle that in a court of law everyone is equal, but in the world of Maycomb, as Tom's trial shows, this is far from the truth.

Makes the point clearly without going into too much detail about the trial.

Well-chosen quotation that supports the point.

Succinct and perceptive point shows Lee's argument.

The conviction destroys Jem's faith in the legal process and in the people he has always trusted. Tom's role is that of the mockingbird of the title – his desire to help Mayella Ewell because he felt pity for her has resulted in his destruction. In the process of that destruction, which has its final act in his being shot by the prison guards, the children's innocence is also destroyed and the whole Finch family only just escape being destroyed by Bob Ewell. The prejudice that grips their community has far-reaching and tragic consequences, shown through Tom Robinson. As Scout later realizes, 'Atticus had used every tool available to free men to save Tom Robinson, but in the secret courts of men's hearts Atticus had no case. Tom was a dead man the minute Mayella Ewell opened her mouth and screamed.'

Shows how Tom's role has wider significance.

Explores link between the symbol and the question.

Shows how prejudice has wider repercussions than Tom and his family.

Finishes with strong relevant quotation that sums up the answer.

This is a well-structured answer that keeps its focus clearly on the question and puts Tom Robinson's role at the centre. It shows evidence of wider reading and understanding of the context of the novel, when it was written and when it was set. It is well written and shows a perceptive response to the author's intentions. It uses well-chosen textual evidence and quotations and evaluates them intelligently.

Sample answer 3

Read the following extract taken from a student response, together with examiner comments, to the sample **Foundation Tier** question:

> What do you think about Atticus Finch?
>
> Think about:
>
> - what you learn about him as a person
>
> - his relationship with the children
>
> - how he defends Tom Robinson.
>
> Add anything else you think is important.

This addresses the second bullet point directly.

Some confusion about the context of this quotation, which is not embedded or explained.

Two different points are muddled together here, but they do show knowledge.

Candidate uses textual evidence to support the point.

Selection of evidence could have been more relevant.

Good use of embedded quotation, although explanation lacks clarity.

Brief, but not explained; mention of context, but not explained.

Atticus has a good relationship with his children. He is quite strict with them because he makes Scout go to school when she is unhappy. I know this because he says

"You never really understand a person... until you climb into his skin and walk around in it."

He wants to make Scout see things from another person's point of view. Also he backs up Calpurnia when she smacks Scout because of her rudeness to Walter Cunningham. He also tells her she must not fight people when they call him names.

Atticus tries to play American football with Jem but says he is too old to tackle him. This makes Jem think Atticus is feeble until he shoots the mad dog. The children are told 'it's a sin to kill a mockingbird' but it is OK to shoot Tim Johnson because he is dangerous to people and he is dying anyway. The children think it is great to have a dead shot for their dad, but Atticus tells them that is not real courage.

Very brief attempt to address the theme of courage.

The candidate shows some knowledge and understanding of the book and of Atticus as a father, but the answer is not well structured and in places there is some confusion about how to select appropriate evidence.

Sample answer 4

Read the extract below taken from a student response, together with examiner comments, to the following sample **Higher Tier** question:

> Look at the extract in Chapter 15 from '*There was a smell of stale whisky and pig-pen about...* ' to "*You got fifteen seconds to get 'em outa here.*"
>
> How does Harper Lee make this such a tense and exciting scene in the novel?

One of the ways in which Lee makes this scene tense is her use of adverbs at the start when she describes Atticus as 'moving slowly', putting his newspaper down 'very carefully' and smoothing the creases with 'lingering fingers'. All of these descriptive phrases suggest that Atticus is trying to give himself time to think what he should do now his children are in danger too. We can tell he fears for them because his fingers 'were trembling a little'. He has good cause to feel afraid as the men surrounding him are a lynch mob, bent on taking Tom Robinson from jail and hanging him from a tree, as happened in other places in the American south at the time.

Another way in which Lee makes the scene exciting is through the actions of the children. Jem behaves out of character when he refuses to obey Atticus's instruction to 'go home'. When Scout describes how 'Mutual defiance made them alike', the reader wonders who will win the battle of wills. When Scout kicks the man who grabbed Jem, she is acting very much in character, defending her brother and she tells Atticus, "Ain't nobody gonna do Jem that way". This is typical of Scout's dialogue when she feels her family is threatened. The reader is then anxious to see whether her action will bring reprisal from the mob, which adds to the suspense.

Lee also uses action verbs, such as 'grabbed', 'yanked', 'kicked' and 'growled' at this point, which describe what is taking place, imply aggression and make the reader want to know what happens next.

Addresses the question directly and makes good use of details from the extract.

Intelligent selection of quotations to answer the question with correct use of terminology.

Good explanation of quotations, which looks at implied meaning.

Relevant use of contextual information to explain the author's use of language.

Identifies author's use of different viewpoints and characters' actions.

Thoughtful point about Lee's use of tension, using well-chosen quotation.

Another well-chosen embedded quotation, which reflects the use of dialogue.

Further explanation of how the characters' behaviour increases suspense.

Candidate uses well-organized, high-level vocabulary and comment.

Some well-selected details of the way Lee uses language, plot development and tension.

This answer shows a high level of skill in the selecting and evaluating of evidence, identifying the author's techniques and expressing all this in a succinct and intelligent writing style.

Glossary

African–American civil rights movement a political movement in the United States (1955–1968) aimed at outlawing racial discrimination and giving voting and other civil rights to black citizens

atmosphere the mood created by a piece of writing

caste system a Hindu system where people are ranked by the social class they are born into; generally used to describe any class system in a society

cause and effect the way an action can cause something else to happen

colloquial language informal, everyday speech

coming of age growing into adulthood through knowledge and experience

dialogue conversation between characters in a novel

disenfranchise to deprive someone of their rights of citizenship, including the right to vote

elision the leaving out of one or more sounds from a word to make it easier to say

enmity a feeling of hostility towards someone

first-person narration a story told from the narrator's point of view, using the pronoun 'I'

gothic a literary style characterized by tales of horror and the supernatural

irony the discrepancy between what a character could be expected to do and what they actually do, often for comic effect

Jim Crow laws a system of racial segregation laws enacted in the United States between 1876 and 1965

metaphor a comparison of one thing to another to make a description more vivid; a metaphor states that one thing *is* the other

naivety innocence

narrative structure the way in which a writer organizes a story to create meaning

narrator the person who tells a story (Scout is the narrator in *To Kill a Mockingbird*)

protagonist the central character in a novel, around whom most of the action revolves

segregation the policy of having separate facilities for different racial groups within a society

simile a comparison of one thing to another to make a description more vivid, using the words 'like' or 'as' to make the comparison

social hierarchy a system where people are ranked in society according to status

symbolism using something to represent a concept, idea or theme in a novel

Wall Street crash a devastating stock market crash in 1929 which signalled the beginning of the Great Depression

OXFORD
UNIVERSITY PRESS

Great Clarendon Street, Oxford OX2 6DP

Oxford University Press is a department of the University of Oxford.
It furthers the University's objective of excellence in research,
scholarship, and education by publishing worldwide in

Oxford   New York

Auckland Cape Town Dar es Salaam Hong Kong Karachi
Kuala Lumpur Madrid Melbourne Mexico City Nairobi
New Delhi Shanghai Taipei Toronto

With offices in

Argentina Austria Brazil Chile Czech Republic France Greece
Guatemala Hungary Italy Japan Poland Portugal Singapore
South Korea Switzerland Thailand Turkey Ukraine Vietnam

Oxford is a registered trade mark of Oxford University Press
in the UK and in certain other countries

British Library Cataloguing in Publication Data

Data available

ISBN 978-0-19-912879-2

10 9 8 7 6 5 4 3 2 1

MIX
Paper from
responsible sources
FSC   FSC® C007785
www.fsc.org

Printed in Great Britain by Bell and Bain Ltd., Glasgow

Acknowledgements
The publisher and author are grateful for permission to reprint the
following copyright material:

Extracts from Harper Lee: *To Kill a Mockingbird* (Arrow, 2010), copyright ©
Harper Lee 1960, reprinted by permission of The Random House Group
Ltd.

Cover: Photodisc/OUP; **p7:** AF archive/Alamy; **p9:** Pictorial Press Ltd/
Alamy; **p12:** Getty Images; **p14:** Moviestore collection Ltd/Alamy;
p20: Getty Images; **p21:** Corbis; **p23:** The Protected Art Archive/Alamy;
p24: Pictorial Press Ltd/Alamy; **p26:** AF archive/Alamy; **p31:** AF archive/
Alamy; **p35:** AF archive/Alamy; **p41:** Moviestore collection Ltd/Alamy;
p43: Photos 12/Alamy; **p49:** Corbis; **p50:** William Leaman/Alamy;
p53: World History Archive/Alamy; **p56:** Corbis.

Artwork by Barking Dog.